VOLUNTEER JOB DESCRIPTIONS AND ACTION PLANS

Marlene Wilson, Author and General Editor

Group's Volunteer Leadership Series™
Volume 3
Group's Church Volunteer Central™

Loveland, Colorado

Group's Volunteer Leadership Series™, Volume 3

Volunteer Job Descriptions and Action Plans

Visit our Web site: **www.grouppublishing.com**

Credits
Author: Marlene Wilson
Editors: Mikal Keefer and Brad Lewis
General Editor: Marlene Wilson
Chief Creative Officer: Joani Schultz
Art Director: Nathan Hindman
Cover Designer: Jeff Storm
Production Manager: Peggy Naylor

Unless otherwise noted, Scripture taken from the HOLY BIBLE, NEW INTERNATIONAL VERSION®. Copyright © 1973, 1978, 1984 International Bible Society. Used by permission of Zondervan Publishing House. All rights reserved.

Produced with the assistance of The Livingstone Corporation (www.LivingstoneCorp.com). Project staff includes Chris Hudson, Ashley Taylor, Mary Horner Collins, Joel Bartlett, Cheryl Dunlop, Mary Larsen, and Rosalie Krusemark.

Library of Congress Cataloging-in-Publication Data

Wilson, Marlene.
Volunteer job descriptions and action plans / Marlene Wilson.—1st American
      hardbound ed.
    p. cm. — (Group's volunteer leadership series ; v. 3)
    Includes bibliographical references.
    ISBN 0-7644-2747-4 (alk. paper)
    1. Voluntarism—Religious aspects—Christianity. 2. Christian leadership.
3. Church work. I. Title. II. Series.
    BR115.V64W556 2003
    253'.7—dc22   2003022120

10 9 8 7 6 5 4 3 2 1   12 11 10 09 08 07 06 05 04

Printed in the United States of America.

Contents

Introduction

Congratulations!

You've taken the first baby steps—well, maybe *giant* steps—toward launching or re-energizing your church's volunteer ministry. That's exciting, and I'm so glad that through these volumes we're able to come alongside you on your journey.

You've demonstrated that volunteers are valuable—so valuable that it's worth involving them in significant ministry. You've proven that as volunteers get more involved, your church will do a better job being what God wants you to be and doing what God wants you to do.

You have a vision and a mission statement. You've got people praying. You've pulled together a task force. So, *now* what do you do? What are the next steps?

Let me suggest five things you'll want to do now—and you'll learn how to do them in this volume.

First, put your volunteer task force to work creating action plans for the volunteer ministry's goals and objectives. Here's a chance to practice your volunteer management skills! You don't need to do all the work yourself; it's time to get your team busy so there's ownership (and so you can take a break!).

Determine the aspects of your church's ministry where volunteers can effectively and meaningfully serve. Good thing you've gotten your church leaders' approval—you'll need their help here as you identify what volunteers will do—and where.

Create volunteer job descriptions. It's not hard to create these essential forms once you understand how to do it—and we'll walk you through the process so you feel comfortable and prepared.

Explore how to manage risks. Risk-management is something both you and your church leaders are concerned about. Let's make sure you address this issue head-on.

Finally, evaluate all that you're doing well, as well as areas where you can improve. Why? So you can take the process full circle yet again, prayerfully finding ways to create an even more vibrant, God-honoring, people-growing, relationship-building ministry to and through your church members.

ONE
Getting Down to Business

What do you expect volunteers to accomplish in your church? And in which areas of ministry? Here's how great planning—and action plans—will help you nail down those details.

Let's imagine that a well-off, well-loved person in your congregation died a few months ago. A few weeks after the funeral, a lawyer visits your church office with some interesting information.

"Mrs. Anderson left five million dollars to the church," announces the lawyer, "but she stipulated in her will that this money be used for one purpose only: to fund several new staff positions for key ministry areas in the church."

Really? No problem!

Then the lawyer drops the other shoe: "There was one other stipulation: The new staff members have to be brought on board in 60 days, and be successful in their positions for a year."

The odds are your church board would find a way to meet that evening in an emergency session. Inside a week there would be a plan in place outlining where the new staff positions would fit into the organization. Job descriptions would be written, advertising done, interviews arranged, and the new positions would be filled in 60 days—even if it took 18-hour days to fill the last opening.

During their first year the new staffers would receive ample training, get plenty of feedback and mentoring, and be compensated appropriately. They'd know exactly what they were doing well, what needed improvement, and how to go about meeting performance standards.

When that one-year anniversary rolled around and the lawyer came to see if he should sign over the check, he'd find a well-oiled, fully-functioning church staff. Why? Because there was tremendous motivation to see that each staff member had what was needed to be effective and successful.

The bad news is that you probably don't have a Mrs. Anderson waiting in the wings to give you five million dollars. But the good news is that you don't need her. If you'll go through the same careful, thorough planning process you'd go through to bring on paid staff and "hire" volunteers instead, you'll still accomplish an amazing amount of ministry.

> "It's worth planning thoroughly for a volunteer role."

My point: It's worth planning as thoroughly for a volunteer role as it is a paid staff member's role.

We know planning is important. We've gone on vacations. We've survived building programs. We know that failing to plan wastes time, money, and energy, and can result in programs that are disappointing to the people we serve.

Are we planning carefully when it comes to our volunteers?

Even at first blush, it's easy to see that there are many places volunteers can do significant ministry in your church. Later in this volume you and your task force will be pausing to look in detail at volunteer opportunities in your church (these are places volunteers *could* serve, not necessarily where they're *already* serving); for now let it be enough to see that you've just demonstrated the need for a volunteer ministry. You may have to demonstrate it again for your church's paid staff members.

By the way, since we're talking about both paid staff and volunteers, let me mention something to keep in mind as you

The Five Million Dollar Phone Call

Imagine you've received a phone call from Mrs. Anderson's estate lawyer. You've got five million dollars to fund several new staff positions. What areas of ministry could use extra staff? Where would you spend the money to add staff?

_____

_____

_____

_____

_____

Now, in those ministry areas, how might volunteers fill those same roles and accomplish those same tasks?

_____

_____

_____

_____

_____

and your task force move ahead in planning how to use volunteers. If your church (or ministry area) has both paid staff and volunteers, it's important that you emphasize the importance of *both*. While volunteers aren't paid to carry out some aspect of ministry, God calls them to be ministers (see the three theologies discussed in volume 1) just as he calls those who make their paid profession "ministry."

Make sure your volunteers feel like full partners in ministry, a vital part of your church's ministry team. Many of your volunteers are investing in the lives of others—caring for children in the nursery, teaching children in Sunday school or children's church, delving into relationships with middle schoolers and high schoolers, or helping adults grow spiritually in small groups and Sunday school classes. Those efforts are vitally important ministry; don't communicate somehow that volunteers are less significant than paid staff members.

> "Make sure your volunteers feel like full partners in ministry."

One way to help keep equity between paid and unpaid (volunteer) staff is to see that volunteers understand exactly why they're serving. They should agree with, and feel passion for, your church's or ministry's mission statement—as well as your goals and objectives.

Also, help volunteers understand that *you* see them as far more than unpaid labor. Interact with them as front line troops you trust entirely to invest in the lives of others.

You've determined some of the ministry areas in which volunteers could have an impact. Let's say one of those is the church office, where the pastor reports that chaos reigns supreme. It seems correspondence is always behind, the attendance record is six months out of date, and the sole paid secretary is overwhelmed.

You're determined to treat volunteers as full partners in ministry, so your office volunteer will have all the training, tools, and information necessary to be effective. The volunteer will have a comfortable desk, reasonable hours, and an invitation to attend general staff meetings.

So what's next? Do you open the office door, throw a volunteer in, and hope the volunteer thrives? No . . . because you've still got work to do before your volunteer can hope to be useful and effective. The volunteer is needed . . . but you're not sure exactly how. You've got to do some planning.

Creating Action Plans

The idea of creating action plans is pretty simple—your task force decides *what* to do, *how* you'll do it, *when* you'll do it, and exactly *who* will do it. In the context of volunteer leadership, planning is when you decide what things you'll actually *do* to achieve your objectives—and those plans become action plans.

> "You're determined to treat volunteers as full partners in ministry."

Looks simple when I explain it like that, doesn't it?

It *is* simple—but so is moving rocks.

I have a friend who once hired some workmen to shift some of the large boulders on her property so she could make better use of the land near her house. She and the foreman walked around the yard while she pointed to which boulders she wanted moved, and she pointed out exactly where she wanted them deposited. As she talked, the foreman carefully drew a map and drove stakes in the ground.

When they'd finished their stroll my friend looked at the map the foreman had drawn and confirmed that the wooden stakes were in the right spots.

"That," the foreman said with a grin as he tucked the map in his pocket, "was the *easy* part." He knew from experience that actually shifting the stones was difficult. So difficult, in fact, that he didn't want to do it twice—so he took great pains to be sure there was a firm plan in place before the work started.

You need similar plans: careful, thorough, and shared with everyone who either has to do the work or deal with the consequences.

In short, you need action plans.

You need them for your general work as a ministry (for instance, you'll need to meet with paid staff to gather information) and you'll need to create action plans for individual ministry areas (for instance, you may identify the need for a church office volunteer to accomplish key tasks). Those action plans for individual volunteers are the beginning of a job description, and we'll deal with those in depth shortly.

> "You need action plans."

Action Plans Defined

As I mentioned in volume 1, an "action plan" is where you determine specific steps to get you to each goal. You think through tactics and sequences of activities, what will happen and when, and what the budget will be.

Each of your volunteer ministry's goals needs a complete action plan, including (and I can't emphasize this enough) *to whom you are delegating the responsibility to achieve the goal.* (We'll explore *what* to delegate later in this volume.)

Through the years I've seen many voluntary efforts launched for worthy causes, but they lacked a plan. People saw a need and decided to do something about it, but because they didn't plan how they'd tackle the problem or implement a service, their efforts flourished briefly and then faded.

Volunteers who signed on to help those causes felt burned, and probably thought twice before volunteering again. People who were going to benefit from the efforts had their hopes temporarily raised, then felt less hopeful than before.

Nobody emerged a winner.

Action plans would have helped those good causes determine how to not just start strong, but also to finish strong. And any shortfalls in money, time, or expertise would have become obvious before reaching a critical point. If you're going to run out of gas, it's good to know that before you're out on the highway.

How Do You Find a Few Good Men—and Women?

When you're creating and implementing a volunteer ministry action plan, be sure to choose people to help you who have some competence in areas related to the goal. You need more than just willingness. Enthusiasm can carry you just so far.

If you were planning to remodel the church kitchen, wouldn't you feel more comfortable if a plumber or an electrician were sitting in on the meeting? They bring practical knowledge to the table, and that can help you keep from making wonderful plans that have no hope of ever being implemented.

It's a balance as you ask your task force to do planning with you. You want to have the enthusiasm of the uninformed ("Let's put the sink on an island in the center of the room—it will let more people help clean dishes") as well as the seasoned advice of the informed ("If we move the sink there, we'll have to put the plumbing straight through the pastor's study downstairs").

If you have experts on your task force, people tend to quickly defer to them. There's less brainstorming and "possibility thinking." But in reality, you did most of that possibility thinking back when you were generating a vision and mission statement. Now it's time to zero in on your goals and be practical in how you'll achieve them.

Your task force includes people who are representing constituencies, so give task force members permission to speak on behalf of their groups as plans unfold. A church staff member may have almost no preference about how the kitchen is remodeled apart from the budget involved, but the hospitality committee representative (who knows the ins and outs of potluck dinners) will have a *lot* to say.

> "Now it's time to zero in on your goals and be practical in how you'll achieve them."

Remind task force members that their expertise and experience is valued as action plans are developed. Encourage people to speak their minds.

As part of your action planning (remember, you'll design an action plan for each goal), let the person(s) responsible for that area help define the details. You've got a task force of the right people pulled together, so let them take the wheel on this process. Remember: Most people are far more committed

> "Action plans are useful only if you follow through."

to plans *they* help make than to plans *you* made. A suggestion you make that might be quickly dismissed as impractical will often, if suggested by a task force member, be given careful consideration. Modifications will be made. Compromises reached.

And a notion that was initially thought impossible will eventually be transformed into a goal that's very reachable.

Action plans are useful only if you follow through and identify all the information you need. . .

Who will take responsibility for implementing the plan? You need a name. It may be a committee who completes the work, but you need the name of the person spearheading the effort.

How will the action be implemented? Be specific-break the action into steps that make sense and can be tracked.

When will each step be taken? Without a deadline you can't measure progress, so be specific.

The cost matters, too-especially if there are discounts or savings available if the plan is implemented in a timely fashion.

If you're a person who likes charts, those that follow might be helpful as you pull together your action plans. The first is bare-bones, and the second one on pages 16 and 17 allows you to plan in greater detail.

ACTION PLAN FOR THE FOLLOWING GOAL:

Who	How	When	Cost

ACTION PLAN FOR THE FOLLOWING GOAL:			
Action Steps	*Review Date*	*Risk*	*How to Measure Results*

Obstacles Expected	Ideas to Avoid/ Lessen Obstacles	Our Success Confidence Level?

When Should You Plan?

Knowing precisely when to do your planning can be tough in church settings.

I've seen many ministries rolling along full steam, burning through people, money, and time, yet without a clear definition of exactly what the ministry is supposed to be doing. Somehow, the ministry leaders never turned an overarching purpose into measurable goals and objectives.

I've also seen that happen with new areas of ministry. Good people pull together to start a ministry to singles or to seniors. They jump in, but their lack of planning inevitably causes them to run into problems keeping support from church leadership, getting funds from the church budget, or even retaining the people they want to serve. Good volunteers get lost in the process. Potential volunteers don't see any promise for their own growth by being involved in a failing ministry. It becomes a mess because planning didn't happen in a timely fashion.

> "Planning needs to be an ongoing and constant process in your ministry."

Clearly, it's not a good idea to do planning too late. But it's also not a good idea to plan early on, then quit planning. When should you plan? A short answer: *Always* be planning.

Planning needs to be an ongoing and constant process in your ministry. That's one reason to loop the evaluation process back into the planning process. As you evaluate where you've been, you can see how needs have changed, workers have developed new interests, or your church has changed. As you evaluate and come up with new goals and objectives, you'll be aware of and be responsive to those changes.

How Do You Write Action Plans?

You can approach creating action plans in any number of ways, but I'd like to suggest a simple, four-step method. I'll briefly walk you through the steps, then provide an example of how it looks in the real world.

Step 1. Prepare

- State your goals and objectives clearly and specifically.
- Collect facts, opinions, and the experience of others that may bear on the situation at hand.
- Consult with everyone who may be involved—directly or indirectly.

Step 2. Decide

- Analyze all the data you've collected, and think through possible consequences.
- Develop alternative courses of action.
- Evaluate the alternatives and choose the best one.
- Set standards.

Step 3. Communicate, Communicate, Communicate

- Determine who'll be affected by the action plan—directly and indirectly.
- Select and implement the best methods for communicating the action plan to those people.
- Check to be sure everyone understands and accepts the action plan.

Step 4. Control

- Set checkpoints to evaluate progress on the action plan—key dates and steps.
- Compare actual with anticipated results.
- Take remedial action when necessary (change the current plan or even change plans altogether).

Four steps—it looks easy on paper, but we all know how simple things can become complex when you start to add people. The good news is that even when you add people, this really *is* a straightforward process.

Let's take a look at how these planning steps might look in a volunteer ministry setting. Suppose a preschool director is considering adding volunteers from the church to help with a weekday preschool/daycare ministry. The volunteers will work alongside paid staff caregivers.

Now let's run through those four planning steps again . . .

1. Prepare

- Goal: Add five volunteers from First Community Church to assist paid staff in preschool ministry.

- Check with state licensing board for limitations or restrictions on using volunteers, training requirements, and background checks required. Call other churches with similar programs to see if they use volunteers, and ask them to assess the strengths and weaknesses of volunteer involvement.

- Ask the preschool director and current paid staff to identify the busiest times of day when volunteers could help most.

2. Decide

- Ask the preschool director, one or two present staff members, and the church's Christian Education Director to form a committee to help make decisions.

- The committee reviews data and information collected in Step 1 and weighs the pros and cons of using volunteers.

Possible alternatives:

(1) Recruit five volunteers who will assist for two-hour blocks, one each morning of the week, during the busy child-drop-off time (7 to 9 A.M.).

(2) Recruit ten volunteers who will assist for two-hour blocks, one each morning of the week, and one each afternoon

of the week, during the busy child-drop-off time (7 to 9 A.M.) and child-pick-up time (4 to 6 P.M.).

(3) To meet state licensing requirements, volunteers will need intensive training. Before we invest in training a large number of volunteers, recruit two people and train them, and start a pilot program two mornings per week. Determine whether, because of licensing restrictions and requirements, a program using volunteers in preschool ministry will work at this time.

3. Communicate

- The committee decides the best method for communicating the plan to potential volunteers and to others who are affected (such as staff, or parents). Options for communication include a newsletter, group meetings, personal meetings and interviews, newspaper announcements, memos in children's diaper bags, and posting on the church web site.

- Once the final decision is implemented, the committee will make sure everyone is informed appropriately.

4. Control

- The committee realizes that part of the original plan in section 2 should include evaluation. The committee will become an advisory board and continue to meet monthly. They'll ask for verbal or written reports from the preschool director to evaluate if the program is meeting agreed-upon objectives.

- The committee will develop written surveys that will be completed every six months by parents of preschoolers in the program and by the volunteers involved.

- If there are any problems, the preschool director can call a special meeting to determine if there's a need to change the plan (for example, add additional volunteers or do additional training).

- After one year, the committee will evaluate the entire program and recommend whether to expand, drop, change, or leave it as is.

Do you see how the objective has been sharpened and focused into clear steps in an action plan? There's no painful detail, but enough information to let everyone make decisions that make sense—and that are based on a written plan.

Why You Need to Stay Flexible

Action plans can be very fluid. Small wonder, considering how quickly circumstances can change!

Once a volunteer is in place, be open to changing your action plans. Agree up front that you'll change anything that you both agree to, and that you'll always do so in writing. This is good practice if you only have a few volunteers; it's *essential* if you have a large number of volunteers. Putting things in writing builds trust because both you and your volunteers know you're on the same page.

> "All of these steps build on each other."

Remember that all of these steps build on each other up to this point.

If your vision changes, your mission statement will need to be reworked. If that happens, you need to revisit your goals and sharpen them into solid objectives. If you change objectives, you need to revise your action plan. It's like a line of dominoes; if the first one falls, the rest will be impacted, too.

While this sounds like it could be a lot of work, don't be discouraged. Chances are, if things change quickly, it means you're headed in good directions. If other changes happen—for example, you set an objective to recruit three adult Sunday school teachers before fall classes start, and your new volunteers quit before they finish their assignment—you need to revise your plans to reflect how you'll retain future volunteers.

And please don't view changing plans as failure. That's very often not the case.

Plans change when you work with people—especially when you work with people in a ministry setting where you need to be sensitive to God's leading and to the people with whom you're working. That's part of the landscape. Flexibility isn't a luxury—it's a necessity.

Consider the Apostle Paul. His epistles are peppered with references like this passage written to the church in Rome:

> *I do not want you to be unaware, brothers, that I planned many times to come to you (but have been prevented from doing so until now) in order that I might have a harvest among you, just as I have had among the other Gentiles. (Romans 1:13)*

Paul was an apostle. You'd think if *anyone* could do long-range planning with some insight, it would be Paul. But time and time again we see him changing plans, rolling with circumstances that appear, and pursuing opportunities that present themselves.

> "Stay flexible. It allows you to stay faithful."

Stay flexible. It allows you to stay faithful.

We haven't covered all the steps yet in what I call the Volunteer Leadership Planning Loop, but let me share all ten steps with you below. You'll be able to see how the steps flow, and it's a linear process.

I should point out that for existing volunteer positions the process is easier because as you loop through the planning—evaluation—planning process you may not need to make any changes at all.

The Volunteer Leadership Planning Loop

1. What's your *vision?*
   (Refer to your vision statement.)

2. What's your *mission?*
   (Refer to your mission statement.)

3. What are the major *goals and objectives* that will help you fulfill your mission and support your vision?

4. What's your *action plan* for each objective?

5. Write a *job description* for the key person you'll need to recruit to complete the action plan.

6. Decide where and how you can *recruit* appropriate people to take on these jobs based on the skills and time commitment required. Remember: The abilities, skills, and passions of the volunteers must align with what the jobs require.

7. Craft a *message* to communicate as you recruit people.

8. What *training and orientation* will volunteers need based on their experience and the requirements of the job? How will you provide the training?

9. What *supervision* will the volunteers require? (This step includes evaluating your own or the ministry leader's leadership style, as well as the supervisory style the volunteer needs.)

10. How will you recognize and evaluate your volunteers? (Keep in mind it's recognition and evaluation that keep volunteers recruited!)

Notice how step 10—recognizing and evaluating volunteers—is the primary way you keep volunteers on board, motivated, and effective. This planning process is a loop; you're never finished looking ahead. And this process recognizes that the best way to retain volunteers is to do an excellent job delivering on the fundamentals such as planning, creating job descriptions, and communicating.

Here's a secret we'll explore later in other volumes of this leadership series: *Volunteer retention isn't something you do as a separate campaign.* It's the logical outcome of doing other things correctly, including recognizing and evaluating volunteers. Note also that action plans (step 4) play a key role in the process. Until you've written action plans, you can't craft job descriptions or find appropriate volunteers. Action plans are *essential.*

We'll talk about job descriptions later in this volume, but until you have action plans you're not ready to write them. You don't know what you're trying to accomplish, so you don't know who you might need to get the job done.

Here's another secret for action plan success: *Don't treat all volunteers the same.* This is going to feel awkward, so promise you'll stick with me until I finish explaining . . .

If you want to see your action plans actually get implemented, make the volunteers who are responsible for shaping and carrying out those action plans your top ministry priority. If they phone, take the call. If they want to meet for coffee, get with them this week instead of next. If they email, reply within 24 hours.

Wait a minute, I hear you protesting. You want to treat everyone fairly, so *all* your volunteers are a top priority!

If you're leading five volunteers, that's probably possible. But as your ministry grows and you're looking at a list of ten, twenty, or a hundred volunteers, they can't all be your top priority. It's physically impossible.

What do you do?

I'd suggest you decide to not treat every volunteer the same.

While you're available to any volunteer who truly needs to see you, intentionally work through those volunteers who are responsible for overseeing other volunteers. If you've placed Tricia in charge of the nursery and she has fifteen volunteers reporting to her, *work through Tricia.* Pour your time and energy into Tricia, and let her handle issues that arise with those fifteen nursery volunteers.

You're not being mean or arrogant. You're being wise. After all, Jesus himself directed the majority of his teaching to a handful of disciples, then let them spread the word from there. Jesus was available to interact with the lepers, the ill, and the crowds of people who flocked to see him, but at the end of the day when he was providing mentoring, he sat with just a small group of disciples.

I sometimes refer to top volunteers—the people to whom we delegate significant responsibility and authority—as "achievers." They *love* achieving goals. They *love* achieving success. They do their jobs well, and they're creative, energetic, and action-oriented. They want to get moving and stay moving.

If you don't make achievers your top priority, they may very well move on without you, and perhaps head off in the wrong direction. Or they may simply lose motivation and momentum.

If achievers find you unavailable (and *they'll* define what that term means, by the way) too often, they'll switch to another ministry assignment or even another church to find a new assignment. Treat these people well! Don't hold them back. Keep their motivation high and creativity going by never becoming an obstacle on their sprint toward progress.

> **"Every construction site needs a bulldozer or two now and then."**

Are there volunteer leaders in your church whom you've neglected in the past? Perhaps you've actually *resented* these people because their enthusiasm pushed you along faster than you wanted to go. How can you communicate with those sorts of achievers that you don't want to lose them? that they're your top priority?

Not every volunteer you have will be an achiever—but those who are may be your next level of leadership. You don't want to lose them.

Remember: Every construction site needs a bulldozer or two now and then.

TWO
Deciding Where Volunteers Can Serve in Your Church

Before you sign up volunteers, you need to know where you'll use them. Which jobs are best? Which are off-limits? Here are the guidelines.

The phone is ringing. The bell choir director wants eight volunteers by next Wednesday. The outreach ministry team leader needs fifteen people to do follow-up after an area evangelistic rally. But the treasurer, who's always complaining she has too much to do, doesn't want *any* volunteers.

And the pastor wonders who you can rustle up to run the annual all-church picnic. The pastor wants anyone *but* Mrs. Eresman, who unexpectedly substituted soy burgers for the hamburgers last year because she's a vegetarian.

Or maybe the phone *isn't* ringing. Other than in Sunday school and vacation Bible school, there's no place volunteers are welcome to serve in your church. The other jobs are done by paid staff who have made it clear: Off Limits to Volunteers.

So as you recruit people with great abilities and skills, people who want to serve in areas of ministry they're passionate about, there's no room for them. They aren't welcome.

What do you do? Where do you place volunteers?

Three Guidelines for Placing Volunteers

In light of the three theologies we discussed in volume 1 of this series—the priesthood of all believers, the giftedness of each child of God, and the whole body of Christ—and in light of my experience, I'd like to suggest these three guidelines when it comes to placing volunteers in your church.

1. Place volunteers where they're wanted.

If you place volunteers where they aren't truly wanted, the experience will be negative for everyone involved. The volunteers' expectations won't be met, adequate supervision won't be provided, and nobody will emerge a winner.

If you're in a church where volunteers haven't been used much, let me suggest this: Look for ministry leaders who are willing to work with volunteers. Start there. Let your success build based on the glowing reports that come from busy staffers who now have more time, more energy, and more opportunity to expand the scope of their ministries because volunteers are shouldering some of the load.

2. Place volunteers where they want to go.

Put people in roles that match their unique, God-given abilities, skills, and passions for ministry. Dropping someone into the wrong job is a recipe for disaster.

3. Place volunteers in expanded placement opportunities.

Okay, you've never had a volunteer do premarital counseling. But could a volunteer handle that role? Absolutely. There's not a job at your church that a volunteer can't potentially fill. Even if the role requires ordination, I've seen many churches where retired clergy are ready and available to step in if needed—or wanted.

> "There are no limitations on where God can use volunteers in your church."

From filling the pulpit to filing the tax forms, there are often people who have the ability to make meaningful contributions. God has given them the requisite gifts; it's up to your church to provide the requisite opportunities.

The bottom line: There are no limitations on where God can use volunteers in your church.

The only obstacles are the willingness of your leadership to use volunteers and the abilities, skills, and passions of the volunteers themselves.

So we're really asking the wrong question if we ask "Where can we place volunteers?"

The questions we *should* be asking are:

- *Is there truly a need for a volunteer ministry at your church?* (The answer is "yes," by the way, for all the reasons explained in volume 1.)

- *Is that need felt by your church leadership?* (This may be true of some ministry area leaders and not others.)

- *Where are the places that ministry need and volunteer abilities, skills, and passion overlap?* (To get this information you'll need to interview both the ministry leaders and volunteers—there's no shortcut on this process.)

Some leaders of ministry areas like children's church and youth ministry have a long history of incorporating volunteers. Even the curriculum available for some ministry areas assumes that volunteers will be leading the programs, and it is written accordingly.

Other areas of ministry have less history—or none at all. Often the pastoral aspects of ministry are delivered by paid staff only. True, performing marriage ceremonies is a matter of licensing; not just anyone can do it. But premarital counseling can be done by volunteers, and so can other types of counseling and emotional care. Sermons can be delivered by volunteers, too.

You can't force a ministry leader to take on volunteers; you need the leader's support and enthusiasm for the volunteer placement to thrive.

But you *can* look for ministry leaders who are clearly too busy. They're ripe for a discussion about what volunteers can—and can't—do for them.

In this chapter I'll tell you about how to approach the maxed-out ministry leader and identify the one skill that's absolutely essential for working with volunteers—delegation. No matter what a leader is willing to do to accommodate volunteers, if the leader won't do *this*—run away. Don't place a volunteer with that leader.

Approaching the Maxed-out Ministry Leader

I've met many people—in corporations, non-profit agencies, and churches—who feel overworked, understaffed, and underfunded. Of course, in many churches, those feelings are completely justified. They *are* overworked . . . understaffed . . . *and* underfunded!

Especially when the economy takes a turn for the worse, churches have to watch the purse strings. Although a church may not technically "lay off" a staff member, sometimes open positions aren't filled and the remaining staff is spread thinner.

Other times, a staff member may see the need to expand the ministry and he or she deeply desires to add a bus route, open a food pantry, or make sure each visitor gets a personal phone call as a follow-up gesture.

But without more people, those dreams go unrealized.

Perhaps that's where some of your ministry leaders are now—stretched thin and maxed-out. They feel too busy, as if they're rowing as fast as they can but still they can't make headway upstream. They need more hands and more feet.

If you're directing a ministry area in your church, perhaps *you* feel that way about your corner of the world. You're frustrated. You need more volunteers. And you're *willing* to work with qualified volunteers. Bring them on!

Great—because establishing the volunteer leadership system described in this book series will help you . . . but first you've got to invest the time to make it happen.

And that may be the biggest hurdle for a maxed-out ministry leader. That leader has to pause long enough to actually train a volunteer. And nothing sounds less appealing to someone frantically stamping out a grass fire than to stop stamping long enough to explain to someone *else* how to stamp out fires.

So recognize that not every ministry leader in your church may be ready to use volunteers. That's okay—place volunteers in the soil where they'll be welcome and where they'll bloom. Start with the ministry areas where the leaders *are* ready and the volunteers will thrive.

Don't miss that point: *Place volunteers only where they're wanted and valued.* If a leader doesn't want volunteers, don't force the issue. It's the volunteers who will pay for your insistence.

And as you talk with leaders who show an enthusiasm for using volunteers, I urge you to gently test their true readiness by working through the following questionnaire with them.

> "Not every ministry leader in your church may be ready to use volunteers."

Ministry Leader Questionnaire

- Do you believe in the priesthood of believers in 1 Peter 2:9?

- Do you truly believe that all Christians are called to be active in ministry?

- Do you believe that God gives each of his children a unique set of abilities, skills, and passions—a giftedness—to use for serving others and to glorify God?

(Okay, maybe you can agree with those questions—they're biblical and it's pretty easy to nod your head to them in theory. But let's bring it down another level.)

- Do you believe that because of their giftedness, the people in your church have something valuable to contribute?

- Are you willing to help people in your church learn where to use their abilities, skills, and passions?

- Are you willing to examine your own areas of responsibility so that you'll begin to use volunteers to do ministry alongside you?

(The questions keep getting harder, don't they? We're not finished yet. If you're truly serious about working effectively with volunteers, then you finally need to ask yourself these questions.)

- Do you have enough confidence in *yourself* to not only accept, but actually to look for people who know more about something than you do in an area where you need help?

- Are you willing to delegate major parts of your ministry to gifted and qualified volunteers—and be thrilled, not threatened, when they succeed?

- Are you willing to offer jobs that match the volunteers you find, including ones with a high level of involvement— jobs that make sense as a logical "whole" and fulfilling position, that go beyond busywork, and that truly offer volunteers the opportunity for satisfaction and growth?

- Are you willing to move from being a "doer" of everything to being an "enabler"? Can you become a good manager and find satisfaction in that?

I feel comfortable asking leaders these kinds of questions, because in my years of leading volunteer programs, I've had to ask *myself* the same questions many times.

There have been times when I've been so busy helping organizations and churches start volunteer programs—putting together volunteer task forces, developing mission statements, setting goals and objectives, developing action plans, designing great job descriptions—that I was too blind to see that I needed to recruit a volunteer to assist *me*.

The single most helpful thing for me in those situations was being honest and realistic about my own limitations. I can't know everything. I certainly don't have time to accomplish everything. Once I admit that, it's easy to see the need to bring in capable and knowledgeable volunteers to help.

I'm guessing that you as a leader also occasionally trip up because of your own blind spots. You think you can do it all, or that only you can do it right. Sound familiar? That's because you're human, just like me.

That's why I ask you to now pause and read through the Ministry Leader Questionnaire again—this time with a pencil in your hand. Answer these questions for and about yourself.

Or—if you're *really* brave—go through them with someone you trust who knows your work style and values. Make notes about your attitudes. Start thinking of tasks within the volunteer ministry of which you're protective and that you might need to delegate to a volunteer. Do any people in your church come to mind who might step in to help you in those areas?

Remember: You've got to walk the talk. You've got to model the behavior you want to see in other leaders. If *you* won't trust volunteers to do significant ministry, why would you expect other leaders to do so?

> "Answer these questions for and about yourself."

And there's another reason for you to make the volunteer ministry the poster child for how volunteers can be effective: It will help you know what other ministry leaders think and feel. You've worked so hard on this volunteer initiative—are you really going to turn it over to a bunch of . . . *volunteers?*

Yes. And because you do, that means the children's pastor who has labored to create a vacation Bible school that pulls in kids from all over town can entrust that effort to a volunteer. And the pastor can trust a volunteer to visit a church member in the hospital. And the youth director can trust a volunteer to pull together the fall retreat.

Placing volunteers doesn't happen in a vacuum. Each of those volunteers is placed in a ministry and will most likely report to and be supervised by someone. You go a long way toward helping volunteers succeed by making certain those

> "Placing volunteers doesn't happen in a vacuum."

leaders and supervisors are ready and prepared to work with the volunteers in their ministry areas.

And two things you can do to assure a successful placement are to help leaders work through creating job descriptions and to learn to delegate well.

Let's start with job descriptions.

THREE
Designing Job Descriptions That Work

What? Job descriptions in the church? You bet—and here's why this step in the volunteer placement process is worth its weight in gold. Plus you'll get step-by-step help creating crisp, clear job descriptions.

I was flipping channels one day and happened on a show that fascinated me. The premise of the show was that a team went into someone's home and in just a few hours completely redecorated a room or two.

Maybe you've seen the show, or maybe you're thinking I'm too easily entertained. Let me explain: I've lived in the same house for more than 30 years. I've done some things with it, but in many ways it's the same place I walked into way back then. I've got to wonder what a team of my friends or family would do if they were unleashed with paint rollers and the chance to move furniture around, knock down a wall, or install a new kitchen sink.

Here's hoping I never find out.

Anyway, when you're watching the team of remodelers get started, it's frantic activity. They've got a limited amount of time, so they're hurrying along as fast as they can. Maybe they already knew what they planned to do, or perhaps they're just wired to plunge right into projects. And of course, they want the best for their friend or family member—the person in whose home they're working.

But once in a while, you'll catch a glimpse of someone in the background who's just standing around, looking lost. This person probably has some skills or he wouldn't be there. And his passion for getting the job done is just as high as the others who are helping—he wants his homeowner-friend to be pleased when the surprise is revealed. So why is this person standing in the midst of the chaos, surrounded by others panicked that they might not finish on time, yet appearing to have nothing to do?

I'm guessing that no one has said, "You're good at sewing? Here, make these new draperies." Or "You know how to use power tools and read a plan? Here, build a desk for the den."

People in churches are a lot like the people on that television show. Some—the ones that seem to be doing everything—are what I call the "Pillars" of the church. Other people who don't seem to be doing anything I refer to as the "Pewsitters." The Pewsitters *always* outnumber the Pillars.

> "The Pewsitters *always* outnumber the Pillars."

Unfortunately, the Pillars in most churches are burning out (maybe you've been one in the past and you've changed churches or "gone underground" for awhile to get a break). Meanwhile, the Pewsitters wander off, feeling left out and unneeded.

It's a terrible cycle, and it totally undermines the three theologies we explored in volume 1. People with something to offer aren't involved. People who have one set of skills are forced into inappropriate jobs because *someone* has to do it. And one after another, the Pillars topple out of exhaustion.

What's a Pewsitter to Do?

Pastors and other church leaders like to blame the vast majority of the people in their churches—those pesky Pewsitters—for not volunteering to help with the church's overall ministry, or serve in any church programs. Of course, sometimes the reason is as simple as the fact no one has asked.

But beyond that, many Pewsitters just don't *know* what

they'd do if they volunteered. They come to church week after week, and they see mostly the same people doing the visible tasks. The same people sing. The same people teach. The same people collect the offering and make the announcements.

And it can be hard for people to describe if they're being left out. It can be tough to express something that may just seem to be an indescribable feeling. They can't put into words:

> "Many Pewsitters just don't know *what* they'd do if they volunteered."

- what they think they're good at,

- what they got tired of doing when they volunteered before,

- what they know they don't like to do,

- what they want to learn,

- where they're being led to grow.

The following is an all-too-familiar occurrence at many churches. . .

Jack had attended First Church for a few years and had decided it was time he found a place to serve. Jack was a banker by trade, and one thing he knew was that he *didn't* want to serve in a financial role. He did that all week long.

But Jack was intrigued by the idea of teaching in the preschool department. Jack loved the years his own children were preschoolers, and he's the big-teddy-bear kind of guy preschoolers instinctively love.

So Jack filled out a survey and eagerly described his interest, his education, and his experience working with preschoolers. He even indicated a willingness to help each week in the preschool class, since he knew how important it is for preschoolers to have consistency.

About a month later, Jack still hadn't heard from anyone at church about his volunteer interests. Yet as he sat down for the worship service and opened his bulletin, he saw an announcement that shocked him. Rita—who already was the president of the women's ministry at church, helped organize the annual missions festival, and sang in the church choir—was being recognized as the new volunteer serving weekly in the church's preschool class.

Of course, probably no one meant to overlook Jack. But the message he likely received was "They just want me for my money" or "I guess they don't want men working as volunteers in Christian education."

And no one meant to overuse Rita, who's clearly a Pillar. But churches seem to burn people like Rita out and let people like Jack stay on the sidelines.

How are you doing with connecting people with ministry opportunities? Have you delegated an appropriate task to everyone who's willing to do something? You may think the answer is "yes," since your appeals for volunteers seem to fall on deaf ears.

But check your assumption using the survey below. Politely talk with people as they leave your church's services. Ask, "Do you currently volunteer to help with any ministries in our church?" For those who say "yes," you can politely ask about their involvement and thank them. Affirm them—they deserve it!

> **"Affirm them— they deserve it!"**

But for those who say "no," ask them which of the listed choices describe why they don't volunteer.

Please *don't* use this as an opportunity to sign people up for existing volunteer openings. You'll need to interview each person and place them according to their aptitudes, skills, and passions to be effective.

Your goal is to find out why Pewsitters are sitting instead of plugging into church programs as volunteers. Position your survey-takers where they can interview people without creating a bottleneck or delay parents picking their children up from classrooms. And if someone doesn't want to participate, respect that.

Volunteer Survey

Ask the following question of every person that passes. Please indicate whether the person you're interviewing is a child (12 or under), a teenager (13-19), or an adult.

"Do you currently volunteer to help with any ministries in the church?"

If the answer is *yes*, politely ask about their involvement and affirm the person.

If the answer is no, ask which of the following choices describes why they don't volunteer:

____ I'm new, so I don't know where I fit in yet.

____ I've volunteered in the past, but I'm taking some time off right now.

____ I've never been asked.

____ I don't know what ministries need volunteers.

____ I've indicated that I'm available, but no one has contacted me.

____ Other: _____.

___ Child ___ Teenager ___ Adult

How Do We Get People Out of the Pews?

You've discovered a lot about yourself and your ministry. Maybe you're now aware that if you had some volunteer help you could be more effective in your area of ministry. You might find people who are even more gifted than you are to accomplish some of the responsibilities in your job.

And that would let you do two things: Focus on the parts of your ministry you really enjoy, and expand the scope of your ministry as you take on new tasks—and as you delegate new responsibilities to volunteers.

And now you hear that many people in your church would volunteer if they knew what to do and knew that someone was needed to do it!

So . . . why don't they sign up?

Let's explore at least part of the solution to this problem. It's the next step in the process of a volunteer ministry: designing jobs for volunteers to do.

My use of the word "design" is intentional. I'm not just trying to use a sophisticated term for writing job descriptions (although it's also okay to use that term). But I like to keep the word "design" in mind because it helps keep the central focus on artistically and skillfully planning jobs that your volunteers will do—and enjoy doing! The more creative and detailed you can be, the more likely the volunteer who fills the job will be content—even joyful—about serving in it.

> "A well-designed job description is an invaluable tool for recruiting the right volunteers."

Essentially, you'll list all the work that needs to be done—the responsibilities and tasks that can be accomplished by volunteers. Then you'll divide those responsibilities and tasks into jobs that are appropriate for various volunteers.

Take this task seriously. A well-designed job description is an invaluable tool for recruiting the right volunteers.

This tool allows you or your recruitment interviewers to do a better job of interviewing potential volunteers. A well-designed job description will help you determine if the volunteer needs any training. And it will help you evaluate the volunteer's performance and measure whether or not using volunteers in your ministry is successful.

What's so important about designing jobs?

Until you can explain what a volunteer is supposed to do, most potential volunteers won't agree to come on board to give you a hand. Nor *should* they—because you aren't ready to put them to work doing something significant.

Unfortunately, when you have 47 kids running around at your youth group meeting or a bursting-at-the-seams Sunday school, it's tempting to recruit volunteers just to gain some manpower. But if they don't know what to do—what you expect of them or how they can make a difference with the people they're serving—you'll quickly lose many of those volunteers.

Recruiting volunteers before you design jobs is like trying to dance before the music starts. Sure, you can start dancing, but there's a good chance that you'll end up out of step once the music begins.

Years ago, when I came out of the corporate world and started leading volunteers in non-profit organizations, I interviewed dozens of volunteers who were leaving agencies.

> "Recruiting volunteers before you design jobs is like trying to dance before the music starts."

When asked why they'd quit, they often answered, "I was never really clear on what I was supposed to do, and I didn't even know who to ask for help."

Agencies had been driven by their need to fill a certain number of volunteer slots. They thought they could simply get people into place and then figure out what to do. Most often, that didn't work well.

It *still* doesn't work well. Not at agencies, and not at your church.

What do volunteers want—and need?

When I started designing jobs for volunteers and writing job descriptions, leaders in non-profit agencies were resistant. They felt that giving volunteers job descriptions took the "magic" out of volunteering.

That one puzzled me. I didn't consider keeping people in the dark about exactly what was expected of them "magical." It was confusing for the paid staff and frustrating for the volunteers.

Some church leaders feel it's too business-like to have job

descriptions for volunteer roles. They seem to think that getting organized by designing jobs for volunteers is somehow not trusting God. But without job descriptions volunteers are miserable. They're ineffective. They're unsure they're doing the right stuff.

When you make sure people's abilities, skills, and passions match the volunteer position, you demonstrate that you care more about your volunteers than your own need to fill jobs. You show you're not willing to toss volunteers into jobs and then watch to see whether they sink or swim.

This might not seem overly important to some leaders in churches. But think how many people get hurt, and even leave the church, because of wounds they receive while volunteering in the wrong place. They fill a job, but they aren't recognized for it. They may even be criticized because they're failing at a job that wasn't an appropriate fit for them in the first place.

> "Volunteers want the benefits that come from having job descriptions."

Volunteers want the benefits that come from having job descriptions. They need the clarity and the knowledge that the position they're signing up to handle has been thought through and defined.

Job descriptions can help you be sure that you're providing consistent service in your church or ministry. They help you evaluate whether volunteers are meeting the standards and providing the quality the job requires. They demonstrate to volunteers that you take what they do seriously and that you don't see them as frivolous contributors to your church or ministry. They help your volunteers understand exactly what you expect from them—what you'll hold them accountable for.

When you put job descriptions in place your volunteers know that you value them, that you trust them, and that they're making a difference in the lives of the people your church or area of ministry serves.

How do you design jobs that fit both you and your volunteers?

So, as you start to design jobs, realize that this process is part of the total fabric of what you're doing with volunteers within your ministry or as a whole within your church.

Take your leadership style, for example. If you're a rather loose manager of people, you can't design jobs that require constant and close supervision. If you do, both you and your volunteers will fail. You might recruit the right kind of person, someone who needs a lot of supervision. Yet your style won't provide enough encouragement, correction, and feedback, and the volunteer will probably feel lost.

Or, if you could be described as rather controlling and autocratic in your management style, don't design jobs or recruit people who are creative or achievement-oriented. You'll only hold them back, and again, both you and the volunteers will be frustrated.

It's fairly easy to keep your management style in mind when you're designing jobs for volunteers who report to you, but what about a job that reports to another person? What do you do then? Does it makes sense to build in that consideration for volunteers who report to the head custodian, a job that seems to be filled by a different person every six months?

Do this: Make certain you cover supervisors' management styles in the interview process. If it's a significant factor, deal with it in the job description. Typically that's not the case, and the issue can be explored in the context of an interview.

Levels of Involvement

When you create job descriptions for volunteers in your church or area of ministry, you're going to discover that some volunteers want very light involvement. Other volunteers desire intense involvement, and still others are looking for every level in between.

To help everyone find a way to contribute, and to successfully recruit the right volunteers to fill the right positions, you'll need to come up with several levels of involvement for various jobs or tasks. For example, if you run a food pantry as part of your ministry, you might have job responsibilities that include:

Lightest involvement: Donate money or food to food pantry.

Moderate involvement: Work in food distribution center sorting donated items and assembling grocery bags.

Heavier involvement: Coordinate the work of volunteers to deliver food to needy families in community. (See also page 83, "Sample Job Descriptions.")

Creating several levels of involvement allows volunteers to find jobs that match their skills, desires, and the level of commitment they can offer. Due to time limitations, family responsibilities, and low self-confidence, some volunteers want to do routine or sporadic tasks.

But volunteers who wish to commit more time and who have the appropriate skills may be looking for more. Also, some volunteers who start at the lightest level of commitment may want to move to a higher level of commitment after testing the waters. Knowing they have this option can be comforting and motivating.

> "It's wise to stay flexible in the types of jobs you offer and how you define those jobs."

It's wise to stay flexible in the types of jobs you offer and how you define those jobs.

Some volunteers are willing to assume very responsible assignments, and for those sorts of positions I urge you to design "volunteer professional" level positions.

A "volunteer professional" position is one that defines the broad areas of responsibility but doesn't spell out every specific task required to fulfill these responsibilities. It also won't specify the time and manpower needed, because it's up to the volunteer to decide how to best fulfill the responsibility. The volunteer selects his or her own staff from the potential volunteers who have been interviewed.

Often, the less responsible the job, the more specific you

need to be with your job descriptions. The volunteers who consider these jobs need to know exactly what you expect of them in terms of time requirements, duties, and details. Also, be clear about what skills are required. These detailed descriptions help volunteers determine if the job fits the realities of their lives.

Remember: If a volunteer has a good experience at a less-demanding level, he or she might take an interest in assuming more responsibility.

When determining levels of responsibility, it helps me if I imagine an inverted pyramid.

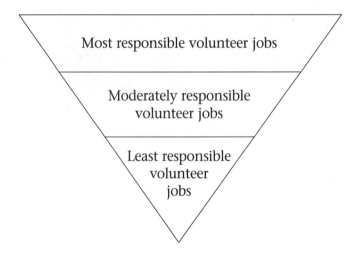

Most responsible volunteer jobs (for example, design Sunday worship experiences)

- Define broad areas of responsibility and authority.

- Assign responsibility rather than specific and detailed tasks.

- Allow volunteer to determine and negotiate needs.

- Define skills and abilities required for the job.

- Leave room for initiative and creativity in how reponsibility is carried out.

Moderately responsible volunteer jobs (for example, create skit to illustrate sermon)

- Spell out tasks fairly well.

- List time requirements and define levels of skill required.

- Indicate lines of responsibility and authority.

Least responsible volunteer jobs (for example, pass offering plates)

- Clearly define duties, time, and skills required.

- List specific tasks.

- Spell out exactly what needs to be done and when.

What Motivates People?

One other thing to keep in mind about designing jobs for volunteers is that the job descriptions need to include motivators or benefits. Do the jobs allow volunteers the opportunity to develop new skills or learn something new about themselves? The worst jobs are ones that are so rigidly constructed that the volunteers feel that they either need to fit into that box, or they'll just have to move on. And clarity counts: I think that the best job descriptions are precise and concise, rather than elaborate or complicated.

> "The best job descriptions are precise and concise, rather than elaborate or complicated."

We dig deeply into what motivates volunteers in volume 4 of this series, but let me briefly introduce a few concepts here. I think they'll be helpful to keep in mind as you work with crafting job descriptions.

When you match the motivational needs of volunteers to appropriate job descriptions, you'll see both motivation and performance improve. And don't guess what motivates people; you can know for sure if you ask them or observe them.

I don't think you can overestimate the motivational power of lining up a job with people's goals for themselves. Why does each volunteer want to be involved in your ministry? Most volunteers will have at least two goals:

1. They want to use their abilities to grow or develop.

2. They want to answer their call to serve others.

As you work with individual volunteers in your ministry, you'll have opportunity to help them stretch. You want them to be realistic about their abilities and involvement, but you also want them to move at least a bit out of their comfort zone. It's a balance—and one you'll need to keep for your overall ministry goals and objectives, as well.

A note: If you lead a large volunteer program, you may be able to provide this level of care only for the volunteers who report directly to you. If that's the case, model how to connect jobs with motivations and encourage these volunteer supervisors to do the same for the people who report to them.

The following worksheet can help potential volunteers learn a little more about themselves and help them understand why they're volunteering. Feel free to copy it and use in interviews or give it to volunteers for self-assessments.

Why I Volunteer

1. As I'm involved in my volunteer role, I want to achieve the following goals:

_____

_____

_____

_____

_____

2. What are some of the positive things that might happen if I reach theses goals?

_____

_____

_____

_____

3. What are my chances for success?
(Place a mark on the following line for each goal you identified)

Very good————————good————————fair————————poor————————very poor

4. Why do I feel this way?

_____

_____

_____

_____

5. What are some of the negative things that might happen if I reach these goals?

_____

_____

_____

_____

6. What could keep me from reaching my goal(s)?

_____ I don't really have the skills, ability, and/or knowledge needed.

_____ I don't want it badly enough to really work for it.

_____ I'm afraid that I might fail.

_____ I'm afraid of what others might think.

_____ Others don't want me to reach this goal.

_____ This goal is really too difficult to ever accomplish.

_____ Other reasons:

7. What are some things I could do so the obstacles listed above don't prevent me from reaching my goals?

_____

_____

_____

_____

8. Do I still want to try to reach these goals?

_____ Yes

_____ No

_____ Undecided

9. Who can help me reach these goals?

Name:

_____

Kind of help:

_____

_____

_____

_____

10. What are some first steps I can take to reach these goals?

_____

_____

_____

_____

11. What else do I need to do if I really want to succeed?

_____

_____

_____

12. Will I take the above steps?

_____ Yes
_____ No
_____ Undecided

13. If you answered yes to item 12, make the following self-contract. Write a self-contract for each goal you've decided to meet.

Self-Contract

I've decided to try to achieve the goal of _____. The first step I'll take to reach my goal is _____. My target date for reaching my goal is _____.

Signed:

Date:

Witnessed by:

How Can You Make Existing Jobs Better?

What should you do about jobs that volunteers are already filling? As long as someone is accomplishing those tasks, should you leave them alone and assume that everything is fine?

That's a dangerous assumption. Most jobs can be improved if you examine them closely.

If someone is filling a volunteer position and is content in the job, you can simply match the job description to the person. But if you have positions that have been tough to fill, or that are plagued with repeated volunteer turnover, designing new descriptions will help solve those problems.

"Most jobs can be improved if you examine them closely."

Ask yourself if the volunteer jobs in your area of ministry are interesting and challenging enough to hold people in them. Ask your current volunteers what they think of their job descriptions and how they'd improve their jobs. Together with your current volunteers, go through your job descriptions and see if you can come up with ways to enlarge, enrich, or just make them more fun.

The following process can help you revise a job description that's not working.

How to Fix a Broken Job Description

Start with a volunteer job description that's tough to fill, or that has suffered from frequent turnover. Use one or more of the following techniques to make it more appealing.

1. Enlarge the job—list additional tasks that you could include in this position.

2. Enrich the job—list functions that might be more managerial that a volunteer could take over.

3. Simplify the job—List tasks that have turned out to be menial and remove them from the job, or combine tasks that could be done more easily by one volunteer.

4. Add variety to the job—Add tasks that spice up a position to make dull or routine tasks more appealing.

5. Create continuity in the job—Add steps that make a job feel more whole; this can add appeal to a position that requires a single task to be done over and over.

Nuts and Bolts of Writing Job Descriptions

Let's assume the worst: You've inherited a volunteer ministry that has dozens of volunteers already serving (that's good!) and you're in need of another dozen volunteers (that's less good) and you have exactly zero job descriptions on file. All the current volunteers were recruited with verbal descriptions of what they'd do, and for the most part they've adapted.

The volunteers you still need are waiting to hear what you want them to do, and job descriptions would certainly help. So you need to work two directions: Create job descriptions for the people who are already serving, and create them for the positions you need to fill so you can place the right people in those positions.

Don't worry—creating job descriptions isn't really all that complicated. It requires focus and information, but you can develop the first and gather the second. And as you'll see from the sample job descriptions below, you don't have to worry about the format of the forms. You can create an outline, use bullet points, or simply write descriptions in paragraph form. Nobody is going to grade you on format or font selection.

> "Creating job descriptions isn't really all that compli- cated."

Just make certain that each job description clearly contains the following:

- Job title

- Goal of the position

- Who the volunteer is responsible to or reports to

- A two or three sentence summary (or list of points) describing the job

- The approximate time required per week or month

- The "term" of the commitment, stated in days, months, or years

- A description of the training that will be provided

- A list of any special qualifications or unique skills the position requires

- The benefits that the volunteer will receive for doing and completing the job.

Use these items as a checklist to be sure job descriptions you write include all the relevant information. Again, writing style and format matter far less than clarity!

Here's an exercise for you to do before you create job descriptions for positions in your volunteer ministry.

Using that checklist, design a job description for your own position. When you're finished, look for areas of your job that could be delegated to volunteers.

If you'd like to see some sample job descriptions, check out those starting on page 83. Note that there are several approaches, and the job descriptions needn't be multi-page essays.

The list of "action verbs" on page 89 may be helpful, too, as you craft your job descriptions.

If you'd like a template that defines what each of the information areas in a job description should cover, see page 90, where you'll find a Volunteer Position Description Cheat Sheet that was developed by my friends and colleagues, Sue Waechter and Deb Kocsis.

And if your church is a member of Group's Church Volunteer Central, visit Group Publishing at www.grouppublishing.com and link to dozens of already-prepared, easily tailored job descriptions for nearly any volunteer position you can imagine.

Gathering Information

If you're working on a job description for a position that will report to you, gathering the necessary information is no problem. You know who the volunteer will report to and what the volunteer is expected to do.

But what if you're in a huge church where you aren't even certain what some volunteers do? What if the volunteer will serve as the associate choirmaster? You may have exactly zero idea of what an associate choirmaster does, and be uncertain if the volunteer will report to the choirmaster, the choir director, or the choir coordinator.

How can you write a job description when you're in the dark about details? The short answer is: You can't. Instead, you need to sit down with the person who will be supervising the volunteer and help *that* person write the job description.

> "Sit down with the person who will be supervising the volunteer and help *that* person write the job description."

That's why it's so important that you become comfortable creating job descriptions; the odds are good that you'll be coaching others on how to do it. I'd like to suggest this quick process for getting busy ministry area leaders to stop and focus on creating solid job descriptions.

Refuse to place volunteers until job descriptions are complete. It's important that ministry leaders understand that job descriptions aren't just paperwork. They're essential for the placement process—and you can't work without them. Stand firm on your need for both the written job description and the clarity and thought that went into crafting it. You're being an advocate for the success of your volunteers and the volunteer ministry if you insist on volunteer supervisors having a clear understanding of what—and who—they need.

Give volunteer supervisors the checklist you used to create your own job description. You're delegating the responsibility to create job descriptions. That means you've got to provide all the information necessary to complete the job.

Give volunteer supervisors sample job descriptions. Use those I've provided or samples from your church. The task of creating job descriptions is less intimidating when you've got a short stack of samples to use as models.

Review job descriptions with the ministry leaders who create them. This brief meeting allows you to clear up any uncertainty you may have about what was written and make sure the job descriptions reflect what's really desired. Plus, you'll be able to thank and affirm the leaders who take time to create job descriptions.

Revisit job descriptions after volunteers have been placed. Six weeks to six months after a volunteer is actually doing the job, it's a good idea to talk with both the volunteer and the volunteer's supervisor. Is the volunteer actually doing what was anticipated when the job description was written? If not, make adjustments to reflect reality.

> "Thank and affirm the leaders who take time to create job descriptions."

Clear, crisp job descriptions go a long way toward getting the right people in the right spots—and making volunteering fulfilling and a boost to spiritual growth.

But another piece of the puzzle is equally important and something the volunteer really can't control. It's the willingness of a volunteer's supervisor to *delegate*. Without the ability to delegate, ministry leaders don't allow volunteers to do anything significant.

Until your ministry leaders master the skill of delegation, your volunteers won't find their ministry experiences as rich as expected, and ministry leaders will struggle with managing volunteers.

Let's deal with delegation next—before you place the volunteers in the care of supervisors who aren't sure how to make the best use of their willingness to serve!

FOUR
Delegation

Before you place a volunteer, make sure a ministry leader is ready to give that volunteer a significant role. These fundamentals of delegation will help your ministry leaders—and you—work well with volunteers.

Delegation is the process of identifying a responsibility and transferring it, and the authority to meet it, to another person. It's thinking through—ahead of time—how to share work.

And that seems so simple—until you try to actually *do* it.

The problem is that it's one thing to assign a responsibility to another person. It's another thing to also transfer the power required to accomplish that responsibility. Most of us are good at giving away the job, but not so good at giving away the power to do it.

When the responsibility and necessary power travel together, that's delegation. When the responsibility is given without the power to do it, that's not delegation. It's dumping. Here's an example of the difference . . .

Suppose Jack is a volunteer in the youth department. The youth pastor approaches Jack and explains that there's a youth group lock-in on the calendar in two months. The pastor wants Jack to plan the program and run with it.

Jack asks questions about budget, schedule, and programming. The youth pastor has already gathered all that information, and he passes the file over with a warm "thank you" and a promise to check in weekly to keep up with progress. The youth pastor tells Jack to pull together the program and recruit helpers; he's got the authority to call any youth volunteer who's been screened and certified and ask that person to help.

Jack has been delegated a task, and he's excited about making the next lock-in both fun and spiritually significant. He understands the goals and has the information he needs to get started. Plus, he's got a weekly "touch base" to get questions answered.

That's delegation.

Now suppose instead that the youth pastor catches Jack in the hallway after church Sunday morning and explains that nothing has been done about the youth group lock-in that's scheduled next Friday. The youth pastor had intended to get things started earlier, but other commitments kept getting in the way. The youth pastor begs Jack to take on the project, and after some arm-twisting Jack agrees.

It's not until after the youth pastor says, "Thanks for saving me, Jack!" and slips away that Jack realizes he doesn't really understand what the point of a lock-in is. He doesn't know how much money he has to spend, or how to go about organizing the event. He's not sure where he'll be able to get information or help.

> "There's way too much dumping when it comes to volunteers."

That's *not* delegation—it's dumping.

There's way too much dumping when it comes to volunteers.

If Jack survives his first lock-in, do you think he'll be back? He will if the task was delegated to him, but if it was dumped on him he'd be crazy to ever take another assignment.

Delegation will make or break your volunteer ministry. You must do it well—and do it wisely. Following are some things I've learned about delegation that will help you as you forge ahead . . . and they're helpful things to teach any leader who works with volunteers.

1. Choose appropriate people for assignments.

Interview and place paid and volunteer staff carefully. This is your chance to maximize strengths and compensate for weaknesses. Seek out skills and knowledge that each person needs to do his or her assignment successfully.

2. Define responsibilities clearly and creatively.

Each person needs to know what he or she is doing. It helps some people to think of the assignment as a framed blank canvas. You describe what the basic finished painting will look like, and that you expect it to fit on the canvas and within the frame you've provided. But the colors, the brush marks, and the decision about who helps finish the painting are up to the artist. This can help the person you're delegating to know where he or she can function freely, and where there are limits.

3. Delegate segments of a job that make sense.

Some positions can be divided more than others; don't assign bits and pieces of a role that won't feel significant to the volunteer. You might function best by delegating a whole area of your ministry to a volunteer. That person then recruits other volunteers to work under him or her. Make sure that those people report to your volunteer leader rather than to you. You want simply to hold the leader accountable for a whole segment, rather than multiple people accountable for bits and pieces of that area.

4. Set goals and standards of performance mutually.

As you develop performance standards be sure to get the buy in of the people who'll actually supervise the ministry area in which the volunteer works. Does the Music Minister care if choir rehearsals start on time? If so, have that reflected in the choir director's job description. And when it's time to place someone in the choir director role, be sure the expectation is clear.

5. Agree on deadlines and ways the volunteer can report progress or problems.

Nothing stalls progress faster than a volunteer being unable to work out problems promptly. Also, reports build momentum for volunteers when they can communicate progress being made, and reporting lets ministry supervisors encourage or correct volunteers.

6. Give accurate and honest feedback.

People want to know how they're doing. They deserve to know. When you delegate, tell people you'll be evaluating their performance and then do so. Communicate that your intent isn't to catch them doing something wrong, but to encourage them to take appropriate risks and even make honest mistakes.

7. Share knowledge, information, and plans.

While you want to allow room for growth, don't let avoidable errors happen simply because others don't have information you could easily share. Let people know you'll be doing this—and how you'll be doing it.

8. Provide necessary orientation, training, and recognition to the volunteers who report to you.

This is the frame part of the blank canvas. Make sure volunteers know their boundaries, but then free them to work within those boundaries by arming them with the tools they need. Look over their shoulders once in a while and say "good job." Talk up their good efforts and accomplishments in front of others.

9. Give volunteers who are capable of accomplishing significant portions of the ministry a voice in the decision making.

Remember, they may know more about that area of your program than you do.

10. Truly delegate.

Most people, when they receive responsibility for a project, don't want you checking up on every step or taking back part of the assignment before they've had a chance to do it. Learn to let go.

By the way, as you think about delegating you'll inevitably begin thinking of people who might be great at assuming some of *your* tasks. When I've served as a volunteer coordinator in different settings, I've made an effort to find volunteers who knew more about a topic or an area than I did. Those sort of volunteers make you look better! If they do a great job implementing a more efficient process, or effective ministry area, you look like a genius because you put them in charge and supported their efforts.

> "Never be afraid of delegating to sharp people."

Never be afraid of delegating to sharp people.

What Should You Delegate?

One reason many leaders have trouble delegating is that they simply don't know what they should let go of. If you're the leader of a ministry area in your church, these questions will help you determine what you can delegate when you find the right person.

This is one of those rare moments when you have a perfect excuse to spend an afternoon alone in a coffee shop or sitting under a tree in the park. You need time to think, with no interruptions. If that appeals to you and you do your best thinking in that sort of setting, go find that park bench.

Another approach is to jot down the specific jobs you do in your ministry work for a few weeks. Use that log to give you the information you need to fill out the form.

If you're not a church leader who'll be delegating jobs to volunteers, by all means have those leaders who will be keep a log of what they do. That will give you the information you need to create volunteer positions that report to those leaders. Or have *those* folks go sit under a tree for half a day as they work through the following form.

And no, they won't *have* a half-day to do this. But remind them that a half-day invested now will pay huge dividends down the road, and if they're feeling over-busy and burned out, this is the first step to their getting help.

Delegation Worksheet

1. What functions—the major pieces or elements of your job—are you responsible for?

2. From this list, what is it essential that you do personally? Put an asterisk next to each of those items.

3. What other things would you like to get done or see done but haven't managed to get to yet?

4. From this list, which of these would you like to do yourself if you had the time? Put an asterisk next to each of those items.

5. Which of the remaining items from these two lists would you be willing to delegate if you could find the right person? Are any of them similar enough to each other that they could be combined into a larger job—something that could be delegated as a whole to give you more relief, as well as provide a volunteer with a meaningful role? What might those job titles be?

6. Considering those job titles, what would the ideal person for each of these jobs look like? What skills, experience, aptitudes, and spiritual maturity would he or she have?

Levels of delegation

Question 5 in the worksheet suggests that you think about how you could combine similar responsibilities to create a larger volunteer job. One advantage of this arrangement is that the volunteer you recruit for the larger job can then recruit others to help fulfill that job. Those volunteers then report to the volunteer leader rather than directly to you. Only the volunteer leader reports to you.

Think of it this way: If it takes ten people to lead small groups in your church, would you rather have all ten of them call you to report how the weekly meetings went, or call someone you recruit to run that ministry? Wouldn't it be handy to have a small group team leader?

If you're like me, you'll opt for a weekly call from your small group team leader. If that volunteer is trained and capable, your ten small group leaders will get great encouragement and support—and you'll get one call instead of ten.

A system that has volunteers managing volunteers requires you to train not just volunteers, but volunteer *supervisors*. If you want to have people in those roles, create job descriptions for those spots. You must be intentional about creating those positions.

Check out the samples of job descriptions with different levels of involvement on page 93.

The Cost of Delegation

For ministry leaders, delegation can feel costly. It requires doing the preparation so a meaningful responsibility can be passed along. It demands thought and planning.

And, frankly, it requires giving up some power. We don't do that easily or comfortably. What happens if you hand over a job to someone who fails to do it—or do it well? How will that reflect on you? How will you relate to the person who let you down?

> "For ministry leaders, delegation can feel costly."

The call to delegate raises some questions in the minds of leaders—including you. How would you answer these?

Can you value administration as well as doing the work yourself? Some leaders find their personal value and worth in being able to do things well. Some fear that if they delegate certain areas of their ministry or program, people might not think they're doing their job.

Will your job be as fun if you just do administration? Many church leaders went into professional ministry because they enjoy the activities associated with the role. Some tasks are fun, and giving them away to volunteers will make the job far less rewarding and enjoyable.

Will things get done right? In the church it's important that things get done properly. After all, if the new members' class is boring, families might choose to leave the church before they form enough relationships to be grafted into the congregation. But is it true that you're the only person who could do an adequate job in that class?

Can you share power? This is the bottom line for many leaders, because delegating is more than assigning a task. It's assigning a responsibility, with sufficient authority to fulfill that responsibility. If you want to delegate well, you must delegate the authority or empowerment that allows someone to do a meaningful job. How do you feel about that?

Good delegation involves trust.

It's a two-way street: The volunteer must trust that sufficient information and power has been transferred. Otherwise the volunteer role will be difficult and will probably end in failure—and nobody likes being set up to fail.

> "My experience is that volunteers want to do their best."

The ministry leader must trust the volunteer to fulfill the responsibility with excellence as it was described in the job description. Otherwise the people depending on the responsibility to be met will be disappointed—and the job may fall back on the ministry leader.

Here's the thing about trusting volunteers: You can generally err on the side of trusting too much. My experience is that volunteers want to do their best, and they'll rise to meet your expectations . . . *if* you're clear about what those expectations are. There's another reason you want to make your job descriptions clear, concise, and achievable!

Help is on the way.

If the notion of delegating areas of ministry feels *odd* to you, don't worry: There are plenty of biblical examples of leaders doing precisely that.

Moses found that it was more than a full-time job just settling squabbles between people, and at his father-in-law's advice he turned over a significant piece of his mediation responsibility to carefully chosen men.

And then there's this example of delegation described in the book of Acts:

> *In those days when the number of disciples was increasing, the Grecian Jews among them complained against the Hebraic Jews because their widows were being overlooked in the daily distribution of food. So the Twelve gathered all the disciples together and said, "It would not be right for us to neglect the ministry of the word of God in order to wait on tables. Brothers, choose seven men from among you who are known to be full of the Spirit and wisdom. We will turn this responsibility over to them and will give our attention to prayer and the ministry of the word." (Acts 6:1-4)*

Seven men were chosen whose qualifications matched the job description, and the responsibility became theirs. That freed the apostles to focus on doing what was most important in their ministry: prayer and preaching. Caring for widows wasn't a job that was dumped—it was delegated. And the results were predictably positive as the church grew.

The apostles realized something that perhaps is dawning on you and other ministry leaders in your church, too: You can't do it all. At least, you can't do it all *well*. It's time to delegate.

It takes some work to delegate—to adequately identify the task, create the job description, and locate the proper people who will fulfill the responsibility. But making the effort can breathe new life into your ministry because at last you'll be able to *catch* your breath.

Delegate well and you'll be surrounded by top-notch people who are there to help. You'll have time to dream of new ways your ministry can develop—and you'll have time to do something about those dreams.

And if the current pace of ministry is burning you out, you'll be able to lean on other people who understand and who have a stake in your being successful.

And you'll have an additional benefit: You'll personally witness God using volunteers who are growing spiritually, finding meaning, and sensing fulfillment as they live out their faith by serving others.

FIVE
The Risk of Using Volunteers

The days of pretending bad things don't happen at church—or to the people our volunteers serve—have long since ended. How can you protect your church, your volunteers, and the people you serve?

It's a call no pastor wants to receive. Color drained from the pastor's face as he heard the news that for more than three years a volunteer in the children's ministry had been abusing children in his care.

It's a call no volunteer wants to receive. A boy in the church-sponsored midweek program claimed that the volunteer had exposed himself to the boy. Although the volunteer knew it wasn't true, a police investigation was underway.

Some risks you face in your ministry are obvious: Your building might burn down. You might have a budget crunch that takes some of your programs off-line. You might find that your attendance doubles (or triples) and suddenly your facilities must be replaced.

Because your church is growing and alive, there are risks. It comes with the territory. That's also true of your volunteer ministry.

But if one of your volunteers does something to a person he or she is serving . . . or if a claim is made against a volunteer you've placed in ministry . . . the losses are more than just a building.

Reputations crumble. Ministry is derailed. Trust is destroyed.

I'm not trying to scare you, but I do want to instill a sense of urgency so you take immediate and decisive action. If you're not protecting every constituency in your ministry—the volunteers, the people they serve, and the church itself—*now* is the time to correct that oversight.

What Are the Risks You Face?

This slim volume can't pretend to provide the last word in how you should proceed, but I can point you in the right direction. I'll help you think through the possibilities and decide on some next steps in your process. And I'll pay extra attention to how you can protect your volunteer ministry and your volunteers.

The topic is "risk management," and it needs to be on your radar screen.

Risk management

Perhaps you've not thought much about risk management. But quickly answer these questions:

- Can a volunteer's acts make your church liable if another person is harmed? (The answer is yes!)

- Are your volunteers protected by law from any liability, or can your volunteers be held liable for certain actions? (The answer is that liability protection laws in most jurisdictions don't fully protect your volunteers.)

- Could your church face significant loss because of expenses incurred from a lawsuit? (Absolutely. And the financial losses are just part of the price you'd pay.)

- Are there potential volunteers who will shy away from signing up to volunteer if you're unable to describe the steps you've taken to protect them and the people they serve? (Yes. It's probably happening already.)

Enough scare tactics

Rather than dwelling on what *could* happen in the area of risk and liability, let's try to come up with some ways to manage and minimize those risks and liabilities.

I think the following is a pretty good definition of risk management: Risk management includes all management efforts aimed at minimizing the adverse impact that losses may have on an organization. The goal is to put in place systematic, organized processes that avoid, eliminate, or lower the chances that a loss will occur.

What's required of you to do risk management is that you identify what processes will accomplish eliminating or lowering your risks, then put those processes in place. Where risk management is concerned, talk is a great place to start, but action is required.

> "Where risk management is concerned, talk is a great place to start, but action is required."

The consequences of not initiating risk management procedures and policies are potentially severe. Not only will your church and ministry be impacted, but individual lives of volunteers (or members of your congregation) can be tragically damaged.

Why Do You Need to Manage Risk?

There's a cost associated with managing risk, both in time and dollars. But as noted above, there's a cost associated with not managing risk, too.

Being found negligent just one time could result in financial damage your church or ministry couldn't survive. With the decline of "charitable immunity"—the legal doctrine that at one time protected charitable organizations from financial responsibility for causing harm—liability for most non-profit organizations is the same as it is in for-profit businesses. So, the primary goal of managing risk in your volunteer program is to create a relatively safe environment where your volunteers can carry out the mission of your church or area of ministry.

How Can You Manage Risk?

Of course, you can't completely eliminate risk in your church or area of ministry. That's why I keep referring to "managing risk." Probably every volunteer and volunteer position brings some level of liability right inside your facility. Since you can't completely eliminate risks, you need to use your judgment and start by focusing on the ones that matter most.

Also, please again note that this brief chapter is just a primer on risk management. My goal is to bring this topic to your attention, to help you measure where you are in terms of risk management, and to nudge you along to get started on being proactive. But you'll probably need additional resources.

If you choose to use some, I strongly recommend *Beyond Police Checks: The Definitive Volunteer and Employee Screening Guidebook* by Linda L. Graff (Dundas, Ontario, Canada: Linda Graff and Associates, Inc., 1999). I also recommend workshops conducted by Sue Waechter and Deb Kocsis (info@cornerstoneconsultingassociates.com).

Where do you start? I recommend that you take these four steps.

1. Look at each volunteer position and identify any potential areas for liability. Again, use your judgment and concentrate on reducing risk in the areas that matter most. These will probably be areas where the people served are the most vulnerable: children and teenagers, people with disabilities, and senior adults.

2. Evaluate the ways you can manage those risks. What can you do to protect the people you serve—and your volunteers? Are you willing to proactively take steps to raise awareness and make changes?

3. Choose the means and implement your strategy. Here's where you actually do something. Be aware that in any risk management strategy, the volunteer recruitment and placement process is thoroughly investigated. Practically speaking, that means when you're in the interview phase of volunteer recruitment (see volume 4 for details) you'll have to decide when to initiate police screenings of volunteers.

4. Monitor your ministries and determine whether the means of managing the risk is meeting your church's needs and the needs of the people you're serving. Make sure the steps you've put in place are truly managing the risks you've identified.

Complete the self-assessment on page 72 through 74 to gauge how well your church or your particular area of ministry currently recognizes and manages risk. The assessment looks long, but you'll cruise through it in about ten minutes.

Please choose one of the three answers; Yes, No, and Unsure (?).
Put a check mark in the box of your choice.

General Liability and Risk Management	Yes	No	?
Does our church have an ongoing risk management committee?			
Have we examined the activities performed by volunteers and taken action to manage the risks?			
Do we have a policy and procedure manual for our volunteer program?			
Do we formally review the manual every year?			
Do we have general liability coverage for the volunteer program?			
Is one person responsible to review and update the liability coverage?			
Do we have events throughout the year that put us at greater risk for liability; if so, do we obtain coverage?			
Managing the Risks of Interviewing, Screening, and Terminating Volunteers			
Do we have current job descriptions for each volunteer position in our church, including board members?			
Do volunteer job descriptions clearly indicate what qualifications are needed to fill each position?			
Do our job descriptions specify what physical requirements are required for the position?			
Do we protect ourselves against discrimination in the way we write our position descriptions?			
Do we complete a background check on volunteers?			

	Yes	No	?
Do we regularly review job performance with volunteers and document it?			
Do we tell volunteers in their initial orientation that they'll have performance reviews? When? What will be covered?			
Do we immediately handle complaints or concerns about volunteers' behavior?			
Do we have written procedures for terminating volunteers?			
Do we provide volunteers with a written handbook regarding the policies and procedures?			
Do we clearly explain who will supervise volunteers and to whom they are responsible?			
Do we ask volunteers to sign a statement that they've received orientation and training and understand our expectations of them?			
Do volunteers understand the boundaries of their job descriptions; what they can and cannot do; where they should or should not be?			
Managing the Risk of Confidentiality			
Do volunteers understand how our church defines confidentiality and privacy?			
Do volunteers understand what they can and cannot say?			
Do volunteers know the consequences of breaking confidentiality?			
Managing the Risk of Personal Injury Liability			
Do we explain safety procedures in working with people?			

	Yes	No	?
Do we adequately post safety warnings for volunteers?			
Do we explain safety in their physical workspace?			
Do we provide general safety training for volunteers?			
Do we have an incident report process for volunteers?			
Do we require volunteers to report any incident that is not consistent with routine activities?			
Do we abide by the Right to Know Act and provide information regarding it? (Contact the U.S. Environmental Protection Agency for info.)			
Managing the Risks of Volunteer Drivers			
Do we have insurance that covers volunteer drivers?			
Do we have certificates of insurance on file for volunteers driving their own vehicles?			
Are volunteers made aware that they must notify us of any changes in their insurance policy?			
Do we need or have automobile insurance above and beyond the volunteer's own coverage?			
Are volunteers made aware that they may need to notify their personal auto insurance carrier of the volunteer driving activities?			
Do we check for a current, valid driver's license?			
Do we check driving records?			
Do we provide special driving training for volunteer drivers?			

If you ended up with mostly "no" answers, a few "unsure" answers, and just a handful of "yes" answers, don't be surprised.

Many ministries and churches utterly flunk this assessment. Don't be discouraged if you see lots of room for improvement; feel motivated. The fact that you're reading this chapter and that you want to do something about risk management probably puts you ahead of most churches!

I strongly suggest that you go through this assessment with other staff members at your church. Bring it to the attention of your senior pastor and your church board. Although they might prefer to just look the other way on risk issues, having them take part in filling out the assessment will help them see how much work there is to do.

What Are Your Options?

Keep in mind that there's no way you'll ever be completely free from liability unless you close the church doors and cease ministry. In our society, anyone can sue anyone, at any time, and for just about any reason. So even if you apply every one of the following methods and many others, you won't be completely secure. But here's a start at how you can minimize your church's liability.

Eliminate the risk.

This is pretty much what I just mentioned—closing your doors and ceasing to do ministry. But before you dismiss this idea, do some thinking. There might actually *be* some ministries in your church that you believe are too risky. There may be a program or area of ministry where volunteers serve, and it somewhat supports your mission, but you could live without it. If considerable risk is involved in that program, you might choose to eliminate that program entirely.

For example, perhaps your church offers a free medical screening clinic to your neighborhood. Volunteer medical professionals use the church facilities and receive financial support to screen for certain health issues of low-income residents. Think about the risks. Professionals are providing the care, and they likely have malpractice insurance. But what about your church?

Could something happen in your facility that you'd be liable for? You might decide that the risk in this situation isn't worth it and eliminate the program entirely. Or if you're very committed to the ministry, you might instead financially support an off-site independent clinic to provide the same services, but with that independent organization assuming the liability in writing. A tough call—but it may be a wise one.

Of course, you probably won't eliminate your youth ministry simply because it fosters relationships between adults and kids. Relationship is a key part of why your church and various ministries in the church exist at all. Instead, you'll want to have enough screening, training, and supervision in place to show that you and/or your volunteers weren't negligent in the event of a negative situation.

> "A tough call—
> but it may be
> a wise one."

Transfer the risk.

This essentially means buying insurance. Or you could use some sort of contract that holds you harmless. Of course, the reality is that even with a contract, you may not be held harmless. Why? Because—as I've just stated—in our society, anyone can sue anyone, at any time, and for just about any reason. And negligence is negligence; no contract removes your obligation to take customary precautions.

But a signed contract, properly reviewed by legal counsel, may help reduce your liability. See page 95 for information that one church requires from its volunteers: a covenant agreement, consent forms, reference forms, interest forms, and a signed contract.

Is it overkill? This church doesn't think so . . . and neither does its lawyer. You'll need to decide for yourself. I'm personally uncomfortable using contracts with volunteers and don't use them—but they are a tool at your disposal.

Reduce the risk.

This means looking at ways to minimize your liabilities by having more comprehensive and up-to-date job descriptions for volunteers, policies and procedures for volunteers, supervision of volunteers, and documented training and orientation of volunteers. You can do this and tremendously decrease your risk without spending a cent. It's doing what you already do (or should be doing)—better.

Some examples of policies that reduce risk are:

- A volunteer driver who takes children under 18 on an activity must have another nonrelated adult along.

- Adults can never be alone with a minor.

- No snacks or food that include nuts or nut oils can be served.

- All children must have signed medical release forms to participate in programs that involve travel or overnight stays.

- Only drivers over the age of 25 can serve as volunteer drivers, because 16- to 25-year-olds have a statistically greater chance of getting into accidents.

Retain the risk.

This means that your church decides to accept and retain the risk involved in the volunteer program, though you do what you can to reduce the risks. This category indicates that your board or church leadership has gone through the process of determining what risks are involved in the volunteer ministry, and your church leadership has formally decided to retain the risk. You'll want to document that your leadership reached this decision.

The good news is that the more you're proactive about minimizing your volunteer program's risk, the less problems you'll face.

The bad news is—I've already said it—anyone can sue anyone, at any time, and for just about any reason. Yet the more you document and record what you've done to be vigilant, the harder it is to prove you were negligent.

Monitor and evaluate.

Periodically check to be sure that whatever risk management procedures and policies you've set into place are still effectively getting the job done.

Times Are Changing

The whole area of managing risks among volunteers is constantly changing. At one time, churches and other non-profit groups had charitable immunity. But that protection has eroded. In the present, your church or ministry probably would face the same liability as any other organization or business.

> "All it takes is one lawsuit—perhaps even one allegation—to close down your ministry."

Because the answer to "What should we do about risk?" continues to change, probably the best tool you can have is a set of guidelines that help you decide what's reasonable to do about risk management.

Here are some guidelines you might want to incorporate into the list you develop.

• **Recognize that the accountability we shoulder is heavier than ever.**

Have there always been cases of abuse by staff members in positions of trust? Clearly that's the case—but now we're in a position to use technology and our policy books to do a better job of preventing people who shouldn't be volunteering from being in positions where they can abuse others on our volunteer staffs. And it's not only *right* for us to take whatever steps we can to ensure safety, it's *smart*. All it takes is one lawsuit—perhaps even one allegation—to close down your ministry.

• **Acknowledge that not every volunteer position requires the same scrutiny.**

If a volunteer will be working at home making phone calls to notify church members about an upcoming business meeting, you probably don't need to do any background checks at all. But if the volunteer's job involves making contact with others while on duty, that's a completely different situation. If those people are children, teenagers, or others who are vulnerable, use the strictest screening protocol you can practically put in place.

• **Get free advice.**

Typically, one question raised in court is whether your church was negligent in providing background screening. Did you do what was prudent and customary? You probably don't need an Interpol screening, but if it's typical for churches and other ministries in your area to do a certain level of screening for positions, do at least as much. Talk with your peers and find out what they're doing. Share that information when others call you.

• **Expect changes.**

Personnel screening is a dynamic field, and the rules keep changing. Investigate and re-investigate at least once per year what's happening. What's prudent and customary is driven by technology and the law; new standards appear with amazing frequency. Determine that for the benefit of your volunteers and those you serve, you will reflect excellence in this issue. If you want to do what's best for your volunteers and the people you serve, you'll stay on top of what's new and changing. Check with the experts now and then by consulting legal counsel and attending some workshops.

• **Establish a paper trail.**

Document every screening effort. Keep information in volunteers' files, and keep files secure.

• **Be consistent.**

Whatever you establish as your protocol, be consistent and apply it to everyone. Make no exceptions—including yourself. Have you put yourself through the screening procedure? Until you do, it's going to be difficult for you to convince others. And remember: If your church is a member of Group's Church Volunteer Central, you may qualify for discounts on background screenings. Call to find out (800-447-1070).

Risk Management Benefits Us All

There are many reasons to be intentional about managing risk.

There are the financial considerations: Your insurance provider may give you a discount if you have certain protocols in place. And you may avoid a devastating lawsuit.

But there's an even more important reason: Risk management protects people . . . including your volunteers.

> "There are many reasons to be intentional about managing risk."

Risk management is often viewed as an effort to weed out predators who might volunteer in your programs to gain access to children, teenagers, or others. And your efforts *will* help deny those people access to your church members.

Yet you're also protecting your volunteers. By adding some risk management guidelines to your training, you keep volunteers from accidentally ending up in compromising—though innocent—positions. If a teenage girl tells her adult male youth sponsor she has something private to tell him, that adult may innocently step into a room and close the door behind them so they can speak in private.

When a parent rounds the corner looking for her daughter and discovers them sitting alone in a dim room behind closed doors, the assumptions aren't pretty, even if the topic of discussion was how the teenager could be more supportive of her parents.

I urge you to create a policy handbook for your volunteers. It's a good idea anyway—an *essential* idea, as you'll discover in volume 5—and it should include material that covers risk management. Be sure you include a statement about which positions require background or police record checks. List what other screening, training, and supervision your church provides. Outline safety procedures. And include a church policy statement on confidentiality and privacy.

You can't be too proactive when it comes to risk management!

(I'm greatly indebted to Sue Waechter and Deb Kocsis for helping with much of the information and content of chapter 5. This chapter is largely adapted from their "Managing Risks in Your Volunteer Program" workshop. For more information, contact Cornerstone Consulting Associates, LLC, P.O. Box 265 Midland, Michigan 48640; Phone: (989) 631-3380; Fax: (646) 349-4985; Web site: www.peopleprocessproduct.com; Email: info@cornerstoneconsultingassociates.com)

Sample Job Descriptions

The following sample job descriptions are from several churches and reflect several levels of commitment. You'll notice they're each slightly different in format, but each spells out basic responsibilities, the essential skills a volunteer needs, and a projected time commitment.

Greeting Card Mailer

Importance to our church: An appropriate greeting card can lift the spirits of someone who is experiencing grief, illness, or loneliness.

Responsibilities: You will contact the church office weekly on Wednesday afternoon to receive the names of those to be mailed cards. You will purchase appropriate greeting cards—preferably with a Christian message—add a personal message, and mail the cards. Costs for cards and postage may be reimbursed, if desired.

Time frame: The volunteer will arrange according to his/her schedule the one hour needed each week.

Skills to be used/developed: This position requires only that you care about people.

Number of volunteers: We need one volunteer.

Benefit for the volunteer: You'll receive satisfaction from letting others know you care during a stressful time in their lives.[1]

(Cross of Christ Lutheran Church, Bellevue, Washington)

Membership and Renewal Committee

Purpose: To integrate an evangelistic spirit into all facets of our church life: children, youth, adults, and worship. Work toward the goal of seeing more people come to know and trust Jesus Christ as Lord and Savior and commit to become members of our church. Give oversight to new member visitations, classes, and integration into our church.

Role of committee member: To ensure that all aspects of our church community reach out to our members and the greater community to invite and encourage men, women, and children to commit their lives to Jesus Christ. To encourage new believers and attenders to become committed to our church by becoming members.

Time commitment: Two hour meeting once a month; committee serves a two to four month term.

Skills needed: A desire to see our church become more effective in witnessing and concern in rendering needed service that may do much to bring people to Christ and deepen the faith of the entire congregation

Benefit to the Volunteer: You'll interact with people who are interested in our church and have the opportunity to share your faith.[2]

(First Presbyterian Church, Bellevue, Washington)

Sunday School Activities Coordinator

Importance to our church: Activities that reinforce the Bible lessons and truths are exciting for children and provide them with opportunities to discover or develop creative expressions.

Responsibilities: You will plan, coordinate, and explain creative activities/crafts designed to enhance the Sunday lessons being taught. You will work with teachers, department coordinator, and resource center coordinator to make sure needed items are available. Attendance at teachers' meetings is necessary.

Time frame: Summertime is a good time for planning, and coordinating is from September to May. You need to be present during Sunday school, 9:30 – 10:40 A.M., every other Sunday. Teachers' meetings are held approximately once every six weeks.

Skills to be used/developed: Volunteer needs activities/crafts skills. An understanding of skill levels for different age groups will help you select appropriate activities and crafts.

Training/resources: Attendance at teachers' workshops, curriculum/activities displays, and browsing through Christian bookstores will provide a wealth of ideas.

Number of volunteers: We need one or more volunteers.

Benefit for the volunteer: You will have the personal satisfaction of using your creative talents in a ministry that reinforces the story of God's love for His children.[3]

(Cross of Christ Lutheran Church, Bellevue, Washington)

Volunteerism Committee

The purpose of the volunteerism committee is to create a more effective ministry of volunteers. A Volunteer Coordinator and Assistant Volunteer Coordinator—who serve for two-year terms—will coordinate and continuously bring together volunteers with committees that have needs for volunteer service.

The volunteerism committee is divided into subcommittees to implement and share volunteerism techniques. The various duties of the committee are:

1. To prepare volunteer ministry position descriptions so every committee member has a clear expectation of what the committee will accomplish.

2. To identify volunteers in the congregation and keep a central record available for committee use.

3. To match volunteers and ministry positions while maximizing the use of all who wish to volunteer and integrating them into the mainstream of church life.

4. To orient and train volunteers.

5. To recognize volunteer service work in the congregation and in the community.

6. To help volunteers experience growth by moving from one volunteer commitment to another through evaluation.

7. To be alert to volunteerism needs and opportunities in the congregation and bring these to the attention of the Church Council and various church committees.

The Volunteer Coordinator will be the primary contact for any ministry leader who has volunteer needs in his or her area. Whatever interest a person may have in the various opportunities in church volunteer ministry, the Volunteer Coordinator will put them in touch with the right person. The church newsletter will regularly list the Volunteer Coordinator's phone numbers.[4]

(Our Saviour's Lutheran Church, Merrill, Wisconsin)

Children's Ministry Welcome Center Greeter

Position Purpose: To provide general Children's Ministry and classroom location information to parents and visitors.

Responsibilities: To staff the Children's Ministry information center during a weekend service. To be familiar with the various ministries available to children weekly and seasonally.

Weekly responsibilities: Arrive at the Welcome Center thirty minutes prior to the start of the service and remain for at least twenty minutes after the service has begun. Place classroom charts, registration cards, and other information on the tables for parents to pick up. Greet parents and children as they come by the counter, direct them to the appropriate classroom, answer their questions, or provide other information as requested. If unable to answer a question, direct the guest to a LifeKids Children's Ministry staff member.

Requirements: A warm and friendly individual who is comfortable meeting new people. An individual who interacts effectively with other people and who desires to be a member of a dynamic ministry team. Acquainted with the expectations of, benefits to, and commitment that the Children's Ministry has to our teachers.

Benefit to the volunteer: The person serving in this ministry position will enjoy seeing how God uses his or her engaging personality to welcome people to our church and to initiate an ongoing relationship with the Children's Ministry, the church, and the Lord.[5]

(Lifebridge Christian Church, Longmont, Colorado)

Action Words for Dynamic Job Descriptions

Use the following list of action words to add action to your job descriptions.

Administer
Advise
Arrange
Build
Call
Care for
Check
Communicate
Contact
Coordinate
Create
Demonstrate
Design
Encourage
Ensure
Evaluate
Experiment
Foster
Guide
Help
Improve
Initiate
Innovate

Interact
Lead
Listen
Mail
Model
Observe
Organize
Participate
Plan
Prepare
Provide
Purchase
Repair
Research
Review
Schedule
Set up
Supervise
Teach
Train
Visit
Write

Volunteer Position Description Cheat Sheet

An alternative "blank" form for designing job descriptions

Position title: A specific, descriptive title that neither exceeds nor diminishes the work of this position. It should give the volunteer a sense of identity, and it should define the position for other volunteers and staff. The title shouldn't distinguish whether the person is paid or unpaid; instead, it should simply reflect the work he or she will do.

Position impact: The purpose and desired outcome of this position should be tied directly to the mission and vision of the church or area of ministry. The impact statement should define how the work of this position will bring positive outcomes for those the church or area of ministry serves.

Performance standards: Responsibilities and duties should be listed as performance standards to be clear about the expectations of the person who fills the position. The list should not only include the activities or accomplishments, but the way the duties are carried out.

Qualifications: The list of qualifications should be clear and explicit. Communicate what is minimally required for this position, as well as what would be beneficial. Include education, personal characteristics, skills, abilities, and experience.

Benefits: This should describe the benefits to the volunteer in this position. State the benefits from the volunteer's perspective, not what the church or area of ministry will receive. Be sure to state benefits, not features.

Commitment required: With the people your church or ministry serves in mind, be explicit about what the requirements are for a person's commitment. How long do you expect a volunteer to serve in this position? How many hours per week, month, year? Address the issue of absenteeism.

Training: Specify the nature and length of all general and position-specific training required for this position. Be clear about what training is mandatory and what is optional.

Responsible to/responsible for: Define who the volunteer is responsible to in the church or area of ministry; define who the volunteer is responsible for if he or she serves as a volunteer leader.

Contract for Volunteering

Volunteer:

I, _____, agree to serve in a volunteer capacity for the above responsibilities for the above specified amount of time and in accordance with the above outlined performance standards.

Volunteer signature_____

Date _____

Volunteer Ministry:

I, _____, agree to provide you with the information and tools to successfully accomplish the responsibilities of this position for our organization and clients. I agree to support you in your efforts.

Staff signature _____

Date _____

Term of this contract:

From_____/_____/_____to _____/_____/_____

Adapted from a handout by Sue Waechter and Deb Kocsis, "Managing Risks in Your Volunteer Program" workshop (Midland, Mich.: Cornerstone Consulting Associates, LLC).

Examples of Job Descriptions with Different Levels of Involvement

Most Responsible Volunteer Position

Title: Volunteer Recruitment Task Force Leader (or Chairperson)

Responsible to: Director of Volunteers

Area of Responsibility: To be responsible for the recruitment of volunteers for this ministry. This includes the organization of other volunteers to assist in this effort as needed; the design of recruitment materials; and the implementation of recruitment objectives, as defined together with the Director of Volunteers and approved by the Advisory Committee

Length of Commitment: One (1) year.

Qualifications: Organizational skills, knowledge of public relations and ability to work well with staff and other volunteers. Knowledge of church and community is helpful.

Comments: This position carries a good deal of responsibility and thus it is recommended that it be your only (or at least, major) volunteer commitment for this year.

Moderately Responsible Volunteer Position

Title: Speaker's Bureau Volunteer

Responsible to: Volunteer Recruitment Task Force Leader

Definition of Duties: Give presentations on behalf of this ministry for the purpose of recruiting more volunteers and encouraging church support of our ministry and its goals. Presentations to be given at adult Sunday school classes, small group meetings, worship services, and at other opportunities as assigned by Recruitment Task Force Leader.

Time Required: 2-4 hours per month. Generally audiences meet on Sundays, but not always.

Qualifications: Public speaking; ability to operate visual aid equipment helpful. Commitment to ministry goals and objectives and a belief in the value of volunteers. Enthusiasm is a must!

Training Provided: Orientation sessions will be arranged with staff and volunteers to thoroughly acquaint volunteer with the ministry and its needs.

Least Responsible Volunteer Position

Title: Telephone Aide

Responsible to: Volunteer Recruitment Task Force Leader and Secretary

Definition of Duties: Telephone prospective volunteers from lists obtained at speeches and presentations to set up interviews with the staff. Phoning should be done from the Office of Volunteers.

Time Required: 2 hours a week. Monday morning preferred.

Qualifications: Pleasant phone personality and ability to work congenially with staff and volunteers.

Comments: This volunteer must have transportation available, as our church office is not accessible by public transportation.

Sample Forms for Volunteer Leaders

First Methodist Church Leadership Covenant

PURPOSE

To agree, as a spiritual leader of FMC, to be "above reproach" so that the world will see, hear, and respond to our leadership in directing them toward the grace of Jesus Christ, and to seek a careful, exemplary Christian lifestyle to encourage other believers and strengthen the church.

PARTICIPANTS

This agreement is for all in regular teaching positions or pastoral care positions, all staff, interns, coordinators, lay ministers, and other positions designated by pastoral leadership.

SPECIFIC AGREEMENTS

1. You have accepted Jesus Christ as your personal Savior.

2. You are a member of (or actively pursuing membership at) FMC.

3. You will work in harmony with the said policies and statement of faith of FMC.

4. You support FMC with your time, money, and loyalty, including participating in the ministries and worship services on a weekly basis.

5. You are known for a dedicated Christian life, according to the standards of God's Word, and you shall purpose to put any sin out of your life that your influence on others might be helpful and not a hindrance (Romans 14; 1 Timothy 3; Titus 1).

6. You are committed to unity, church teamwork, and biblical respect for church leadership (Philippians 2:1-4; Hebrews 13:7, 17).

7. You recognize, accept, pursue, and hold in highest regard the biblical instruction concerning family and marriage responsibility (Ephesians 5:22–6:4; Colossians 3:18-24; 1 Peter 3:1-7).

8. You are careful even in areas of Christian liberty or where the Bible is silent.

THE FMC LEADERSHIP COVENANT

Explanation Concerning the Principle of Influence

Recognizing the responsibilities of both individuals and the community of believers, it is necessary that there be a mutual commitment within the body to certain standards of behavior in order to effectively accomplish the church's purpose (Philippians 3:15-17).

Although certain practices and attitudes are clearly prohibited in Scripture, others are simply matters of taste and discretion (Romans 14:1-6). The church recognizes the problems of Christian liberty, especially within the sphere of those things which may not, of themselves, be either good or bad. Even committed Christians may disagree in these areas.

We want to focus on the positive. Our message is Christ, the cross, and what is clear in Scripture. Concentrating on side issues could sideline us. But we do believe spiritual leaders should show extra care because of their influence on others. We ask that those in leadership and influential positions be obedient to the Lord and growing in maturity. That is the main thing. Then even in areas of debate or Christian liberty, we ask leaders to live with Paul's attitude of concern to build and not hurt others (Romans 14:19-20).

Leaders are asked to abstain from the use of tobacco and the use of non-medicinal narcotic or hallucinogenic drugs and intoxicating alcoholic beverages (because of the principle to guard one's physical body as God's temple) and to avoid the connection with habits considered inappropriate for people in leadership in a church like ours. It is expected of our leaders to live within their means and practice financial integrity.

In other areas of choice such as music or entertainment, eating habits, movies, television, or reading material, those in spiritual leadership at FMC are asked to exercise careful Christian discretion.

Choices should be guided by these principles: done in faith

(Roman 14:22-23) with clear conscience (Acts 24:16), for the glory of God (1 Corinthians 10:31), and to build, not offend others (Romans 14:21).

In areas of possible question not covered here, spiritual leaders are to abide by the direction of the pastoral leadership.

Of course, the observing of these principles does not comprise the whole of one's responsibility to God and therefore does not indicate that one is living under the Lordship of Christ. FMC, however, appreciates the willingness to follow these guidelines because it shows a maturity and spiritual concern for the whole Christian community, and that is a special and larger issue.

NAME (Please Print)_____

DATE _____

SIGNATURE_____

First Methodist Church

BACKGROUND INVESTIGATION CONSENT

I, (Print Name) _____
hereby authorize First Methodist Church's pastor in the area
of requested employment or volunteering, and the Director of
Finance and Administration Office, to make an independent
investigation of my background, references, character, past
employment, education, criminal or police records, including
those by both public and private organizations and all public
records for the purpose of confirming the information contained on my application or volunteer form(s), and/or obtain-
ing other information which may be material to my
qualifications for employment or as a volunteer now and, if
applicable, during the tenure of my employment or as a volunteer with First Methodist Church.

I release FMC, and any person or entity which provides
information pursuant to this authorization, from any and all
liabilities, claims or lawsuits in regards to the information
obtained from any and all of the above referenced sources
used.

The following is my true and *complete* legal name, and all
information is true and correct to the best of my knowledge:

Full Name (Printed)

Phone #

Maiden Name or Other Names Used

Present Address

Length of time at present address

City/State

ZIP

Former Address

Length of time at former address

City/State

Zip

Date of Birth

Social Security Number

Driver's License #

State of License

Signature

Date

NOTE: The above information is required for identification purposes only, and is in no manner used as qualifications for employment or placement.

First Methodist Church

What Floats Your Boat Sheet

Your supervisor wants to get to know you! Give us some insight by completing this fun sheet, please.

Name:

1. What motivates you? (Write three or four lines on how you like to be encouraged.)

   _____

   _____

   _____

2. A daily encouragement for me would be:

   _____

   _____

3. If I could select a gift for myself for under $20, it would be:

   _____

   _____

4. If I had all day to do something for myself, I would:

   _____

   _____

5. The most fun I ever had was when:

   _____

   _____

6. My favorite hobby is:

_____

_____

_____

7. My greatest passion in life is:

_____

_____

_____

_____

8. One area where I am growing is:

_____

_____

_____

9. The greatest strength I possess is:

_____

_____

_____

_____

First Methodist Church

Children and Youth Ministry Volunteer Team Questionnaire

Legal Name (Last, First, Middle)

Nickname

Home phone

Work phone

Cell/pager

Best time/place to call

E-mail address

Street address

City/State/ZIP

How long at your present address?

If less than five years, give previous address and number of years:

Previous address

Years there

__Male __Female

Date of birth ____/____/____

Marital status

If married, spouse's name

Number of children

Ages

Emergency Contact
Name

Relationship

Phone number

Occupation

Place of employment

Number of years

Employment history for last five years:
Employer's name/phone

Employer's name/phone

Employer's name/phone

Do you have a personal relationship with Jesus Christ? Describe briefly.

_____

_____

_____

_____

How long have you attended First Methodist Church (FMC)?

_____

List any leadership/volunteer experience you've had with children/youth:

_____

_____

_____

List any training/education that has prepared you to work with children/youth:

_____

_____

_____

List any other FMC ministries you're involved in:

_____

_____

Age/grade preference

Hour preference

Local Personal References
(must be 18 years old and not related to you)

Name

Relationship

Address

Phone

Comments (staff use)

_____

_____

Name

Relationship

Address

Phone

Comments (staff use)

_____

_____

Name

Relationship

Address

Phone

Comments (staff use)

_____

_____

Applicant's Statement

I hereby authorize FMC to verify all information contained in this application with any references, my past or present employers, or any other appropriate personnel at my present or past employers, churches, or other organizations and any individuals to disclose any and all information to FMC. I release all such persons or entities from liability that may result or arise from FMC's collections of all such evaluations or information or its consideration of my application.

Should my application be accepted, I agree to follow the policies of FMC and to refrain from unscriptural conduct in the performance of my services on behalf of the church.

I understand that the personal information will be held confidential by the church staff.

Applicant's signature

Date

How to Establish a Volunteer Ministry Budget

What does it cost to create and maintain a volunteer ministry? You may well be asked, and this handy worksheet will help you determine what your church can expect to spend. Keep in mind that even if you're using an office in the church and the church copier, there are costs associated with that overhead. Play fair: Roll the appropriate prorated expenses into your budget.

And to keep things simple, figure annual costs. That's typically how church budgets are figured—though it's smart to check.

Personnel

Volunteer manager   _____

Secretary   _____

Additional staff   _____

_____   _____

_____   _____

Benefits (estimate at _____% of total salaries)   _____

Subtotal—Personnel $_____

Overhead

Some of the items below are one-time purchases you'll need to make to set up an office. Others are line items you'll carry throughout the year.

Office furniture and equipment

Desks, chairs, lamps, etc.

File cabinets	_____
Bulletin boards, white boards	_____
Computer equipment	_____
Audio-visual equipment	_____
Additional equipment	_____
_____	_____
_____	_____
_____	_____

Subtotal—Office furniture and equipment $_____

Telephone

Installation	$_____
Monthly service charge (x12)	_____
Long distance (x12)	_____
Message service charges	_____

Subtotal—Telephone $_____

Office Supplies/Expenses

Rent   _____

Utilities   _____

Office & maintenance supplies   _____

Photocopying   _____

Printing   _____
    (stationery, brochures, etc.)

Postage   _____

Subtotal—Office supplies/Expenses $_____

Travel

Local   _____
    (Mileage reimbursement, etc.)

Long distance travel   _____
    (conferences, professional development)

Subtotal—Travel $_____

Risk Management Screenings

Subtotal—Risk Management $_____

Development and Training

Registration fees _____

(for conferences, seminars, etc.)

Journal subscriptions, books, etc. _____

Membership fees _____

(for professional associations)

Handouts/books for training _____

Refreshments _____

Other training materials _____

(slides, films, etc.)

Other _____ _____

Subtotal—Development Training $ _____

Sources

I'm deeply indebted to Augsburg Publishing House for its willingness to let me draw material from my book, *How to Mobilize Church Volunteers* (Minneapolis: Augsburg Publishing House, 1983) for this volume. I also frequently referred to my book, *The Effective Management of Volunteer Programs* (Boulder, Colo.: Volunteer Management Associates, 1976).

Happily, the principles I thought timeless years ago still apply—but I've taken the liberty of updating the information and filtering it through my subsequent years of experience.

1. *Volunteer Ministry: Your Gift of Christian Service* (Bellevue, Wash.: Cross of Christ Lutheran Church, 1988), p. 61.

2. *Serve God by Sharing, Caring, Serving* (Bellevue, Wash.: First Presbyterian Church of Bellevue), p. 10.

3. *Volunteer Ministry: Your Gift of Christian Service*, p. 33.

4. *Volunteers in Christ Reference Guide* (Merrill, Wis.: Our Saviour's Lutheran Church, 1984), p. 17.

5. Lifebridge Christian Church, Longmont, Colorado.

All aboard!

Group's CHURCH VOLUNTEER CENTRAL

Your Volunteer Idea Depot!

Group's Church Volunteer Central is an association that provides busy church leaders the tools they need to make the most of their volunteers. Membership includes 24/7 access to www.churchvolunteercentral.com for:

- Field-tested ideas for recruiting, training, motivation, and retention.
- A biblical approach to volunteer administration, including practical applications.
- Easy-to-use tools like job descriptions, applications, policies & procedures, interview forms, staff handbooks, clip art, e-cruiting, and standardized forms.
- Training for specific positions, self-graded evaluations, and a church certificate program.

You'll also get:
- Discounted background checks and detailed guidelines.
- Discounts on Group's volunteer resources and training events.
- Free phone consultations for volunteer challenges.

Maximize your volunteers the easy way!
Call 1-800-747-6060, ext. 1323

Equipping Churches for Volunteer Effectiveness
www.churchvolunteercentral.com